MALCOLM MUGGERIDGE
My Life in Pictures

MALCOLM MUGGERIDGE
My Life in Pictures

Bliss was it in that dawn to be alive
But to be *old* is very heaven.
                    after Wordsworth

The Herbert Press

Published in Great Britain 1987 by
The Herbert Press Limited, 46 Northchurch Road, London N1 4EJ

Edited by John Bright-Holmes
Designed by Pauline Harrison
Printed and bound in Great Britain by Jolly & Barber Ltd, Rugby

British Library Cataloguing in Publication Data

Muggeridge, Malcolm
Malcolm Muggeridge: my life in pictures.
1. Muggeridge, Malcolm——Portraits
2. Authors, English——20th century——
Portraits 3. Journalists——England——
Portraits
I. Title
070'.92'4   PR6025.U5Z/

ISBN 0 906969 60 3

Contents

I would like to express my gratitude
to two people who have helped me with this book—
John Bright-Holmes who has assisted me with the text,
and Chris Barham, of the *Daily Mail*,
who also lives in Robertsbridge,
for his practical help and his special skill
as a photographer.

Dr Johnson used to say that there were three books he wished were longer: Bunyan's *Pilgrim's Progress*; Defoe's *Robinson Crusoe*; and Cervantes' *Don Quixote*.

I agree with him especially about *Don Quixote* (even though it has its longueurs). It is a sublime example of comedy at its best for, although the Knight's adventures are the sort that everyone wants to experience, they fill him not with happiness but with woe. What is funny is not so much that he is tilting at windmills, but that he is learning how his optimism about life is unjustified; that its lessons are sad ones; that his optimism will actually rebound on him. Hence my fondness for Picasso's rendering, a reproduction of which hangs in my home.

Without portraying the Knight's countenance, it movingly recreates a theme which to me is a constant fascination, and ever-present in life.

I found it strongly illustrated in the character and appearance of George Orwell (whose tallness and thinness seemed to emphasize it). I sense it too in Graham Greene and feel it also in myself. Graham I have described as a saint trying to be a sinner, and I see my life in part as a sinner trying to be a saint. Alas for human ambitions!

EARLY DAYS

I was born on 24 March 1903 in Broomhall Road, Sanderstead, South Croydon. In a similar house nearby two elderly ladies used to run an Infants' school and it was there I was first taught my letters.

ABOVE AND OPPOSITE PAGE A photograph known in our family as 'Mellin's Food'. I was much plumper and better covered in those days than later on – hence this well-fed study which won an advertising competition prize. And there was a 'Mellin's Food'! – see this old Brighton tram.

ABOVE This is me, sitting middle front, at the age of four with my mother (centre) and her sister, and my brothers Douglas (right), Stanley (above him), and Eric, the baby. I am clutching a boat given me by some stranger on the beach at Shoreham in Sussex where this picture was taken.

BELOW I am on the right, aged five, with Stanley (centre) and Eric at our home.

My father, H.T. Muggeridge, grew up in Penge. He left school in 1877 at thirteen, which was possible then if you were clever, and became an office boy at the shirt-making firm of MacIntyre, Hogg, Marsh & Co. in the City. He used to travel to London each day on the 'working-man's train'. It was cheaper, but it used to get him in long before the office opened.

In time, my father rose to become the Company Secretary; and he was offered a directorship. This was coupled, however, with a request that he give up his political activities and this he was unable to accept.

He never did give up politics – indeed he became Labour MP for Romford in 1929–31. Nor, towards the end of his life, did he repudiate his socialist position, not even after the Ramsay MacDonald National Government lost him his seat. Yet I always had a sense of his being disillusioned.

Unexpectedly in so concerned and business-like a man, my father was at heart a great romantic. This used to come out, to my mother's dismay and annoyance, in some of the things he bought for the house: a red 'cosy-corner' which had looked much better in the pub where he found it; and the epergne (decorative table centre) which he gave to my mother as a silver-wedding gift. That he did take back and exchange, but for what I cannot recall.

Mrs Booler, my mother's mother. If she were living to-day, in the 1980s, she would be dependent on government money, supplementary benefit etc. To her, that idea was the last stage in degradation. I have never forgotten her independence and sturdiness. Once I made fun of the Book of Daniel, questioning its literal truthfulness. 'If *Daniel* isn't true', said my grandmother, 'nothing is true.'

My grandmother came from Sheffield, as did my mother. She, working-class herself, always used to en-quire, whenever there was a knock at the front door, 'Is it a workman?' But she was less strict than my grandmother, as succeeding generations tend to be.

OPPOSITE My father and mother, with my brother Eric and a friend, in our garden in Croydon.

12

From as early as I can remember, my father was involved in and with politics. He was a founder-member of the Fabian Society; and would always make a firm distinction between the role of the State and that of the Monarch. The Royal Navy, for example, belonged to His Majesty, as did HMSO; but the *National* Debt was not His Majesty's! It always got a laugh at meetings.

Our household was saturated with politics. Before the First World War, this was something a bit unusual. Our opinions were always regarded as 'advanced' – and I myself gained strong views at a remarkably early age. We used to entertain members of the Fabian Society when they visited Croydon; and my father knew H.G. Wells and corresponded with Bernard Shaw. We tended to think, on the other hand, that Fabian Society women were funny: not only were their dresses as 'advanced' as our views (and theirs), but they wore no stays. My mother, who regarded politics as strictly for men, used to keep a very sharp eye on these 'advanced' ladies.

My father always had great sympathy for socialists. He spoke frequently at the Quaker Meeting House, and possessed an eloquence and a charisma as great as any music-hall star. On these occasions he would suddenly remember one of the prime purposes of the meeting and announce endearingly: 'Oh, we've forgotten to send round the plate.' He later became the first Socialist member of Croydon Borough Council. Opposite is one of his earliest Election posters.

THE SHOPKEEPER AND THE LABOUR MAN.

"Trade follows the Agitator."—JOHN BURNS.

L.M. You believe that the Labour policy is detrimental to your interests as a trader. Would you tell me on what sort of people your trade depends?

S.K. Chiefly working people.

L.M. I thought so. Have you realised that the Labour policy is aimed at increasing the purchasing power of poor people?

S.K. That is all very well, but it means high rates, and that is where the shoe pinches.

L.M. You do not object to spending money where a good return can be secured.

S.K. Of course not.

L.M. Well, have you considered that, wisely expended, what you pay in rates pays you better, pound for pound, than any other payment you make?

S.K. There is something in that. I can see the difference between rates and rent. But how about municipal trading? That must be opposed to my interests.

L.M. Are you sure of that? Would you be better off if the trams, electricity and water were in private hands?

S.K. No; I agree with that; but they are monopolies. I was thinking of competition.

L.M. And you have to! How much longer do you think you will be able to survive against the competition of the multiple-shop companies—particularly with rising prices and the markets against you? They try to scare you about municipal enterprise, because it is directed against them. Tell me, if you found you could no longer continue as an independent trader, by whom would you sooner be taken over—the municipality or the private trust?

S.K. I expect I should get better treatment from the public.

L.M. If you will excuse my saying so, you shopkeepers are extraordinarily blind to your own public interests.

S.K. How do you mean?

L.M. You were complaining just now about high rates. The patience of the shopkeeper under a system of local taxation which presses upon him with merciless injustice passes my comprehension. You will agree that all taxation should be adjusted to income. Have you calculated how much in the £ of your net income—hard-earned—you have to pay in local taxation, and compared it with the local tax paid by a man with an unearned income four times as large? The fact is that the premises occupied bear very little relation to taxable capacity, and form a grotesquely unfair basis of assessment for local taxation, especially in the case of shopkeepers who are taxed on the tool of their industry—their shop.

S.K. What you say is quite true. But what would the Labour Party do?

L.M. One thing it would not do; it would not tax shopkeepers, as the chief consumers of electricity, in order to relieve other ratepayers of their proper contributions. But it would press for a readjustment of local taxation, which would put it upon an equitable basis, and relieve industry of the crushing burden of the present system. Further, it would use all the powers that local authorities can exercise to improve the standard of life of the working people, and—believe me—all that makes for a brighter and happier town cannot fail to improve the position of the shopkeeper.

S.K. That is an inspiring ideal, and I have much sympathy with it.

VOTE FOR MUGGERIDGE!

Wednesday, Nov. 1st, 1911.

Printed at the Portland Press (T U.), 90, Portland Road, South Norwood, and Published by A. Jenner, 24, Cuthbert Road, Croydon.

A group of senior boys at Croydon Secondary School, 1919, myself far left.

At my elementary school in Deering Road I particularly remember one of the teachers, Miss Corke. She was an up-and-coming emancipated lady who, in later years, used to sum me up to my wife Kitty by saying that I was 'a very charming boy, but impossible'.

She was not the sort of teacher, however, who is limited to the classroom. She had plenty of interests outside the school. In particular there was a teacher at a nearby school with whom she had an affair. His name was D.H. Lawrence. I have always felt, from the way Lawrence wrote about sex in his novels, that he must have been impotent. I asked Miss Corke in old age whether that could be true, but she would not be drawn.

At the outset of the First World War in 1914 there was a march through Croydon proclaiming 'Hurrah for War!' My elder brothers joined up, Douglas in the Inns of Court Regiment, later to be commissioned in the Army; Stanley joined the RFC as a skilled mechanic. I envied them, but when I went to a recruiting office I was told that eleven was too young! But the enthusiasm for the war cooled down as the casualty lists grew, and I vividly remember poor Douglas writing home in a terrible state of mind after he had killed an enemy soldier.

When I was twelve I won a scholarship to the new (Croydon) Borough Secondary School, later Selhurst Grammar School. After this we moved from Broomhall Gardens to the more respectable Birdhurst Gardens, no. 17. The school was housed in the Polytechnic, but what with the severe shortage of schoolmasters our curriculum suffered. My academic record was undistinguished; even so, I was luckily able to gain entry to Cambridge.

At the age of 17, in 1920, I fell in love for the first time. From the moment I met Dora Pitman on a municipal tennis court, the whole of existence for me was concentrated on that one face, uniquely beautiful, as it seemed, and distinct from all other faces.

Myself as an undergraduate and taking my degree in 1924.

I went up to Cambridge in 1920 as a Natural Scientist and was even given a Bursary. But I had chosen the subject not for any aptitude or liking for it, but because it was the only matriculation course available at my school. However, and looking ahead to my future tastes and occupations, I did eventually manage a 'Special' degree in English Literature – a 'Special' is, of course, not specially good, rather 'not a scandal'.

I went to Selwyn College, not a fashionable choice, but one dominated by its emphasis on theology. I took up rowing, but the Selwyn Fourth Boat's only distinction was to get double-over-bumped right off the river despite the energetic coaching of Alec Vidler, by then in his fourth year. Despite our difference in age we became friends in my Freshman year and remain close friends to this day.

I also joined a society called The Friars, a discussion group, and became its President.

In my last (fourth) year I took a teaching diploma. Since we were taught by a Mr Fox we were all referred to as 'Fox's Martyrs'. Another 'martyr' in the group after me was the broadcaster Alistair Cooke.

In this last year I shared rooms with Leonard Dobbs, of the well-known skiing family (see over), and it was through him that I met his sister Kitty, a champion skier herself, and whom I now saw with increasing frequency.

OPPOSITE ABOVE The Selwyn College Fourth Boat with Alec Vidler, centre, with loud-hailer. The boatman behind him, whose name unfortunately I have forgotten, bears an astonishing resemblance to Alec when much older.

OPPOSITE BELOW The Friars, Lent Term 1923, with myself, in glasses, seated centre.

A FAMILY OF RACERS.

(1) G. C. Dobbs.
Villars Golden Ski, 1908.

(2) Miss Kitty Dobbs.
Lady Ski Champion, 1924.

(3) Leonard Dobbs.
Cross Country Champion, 1921–23–24.
Anglo-Swiss Cup, 1926.

(4) W. R. Dobbs.
Ski-Running Champion, 1926.

(5) P. Dobbs.
2nd, Championship Race, 1921.

(6) R. H. Dobbs.
Raced for Cambridge.
Richardet Cup.
Anglo-Swiss Race, 1926.

The Dobbs family, a family of racers indeed. Kitty's father George, a Protestant Irishman, had helped Sir Henry Lunn in the creation of his family travel business because he spoke many languages and got on well with the hoteliers in Europe. This 'family illustration' is taken from *A History of Ski-ing* (OUP, 1927) by Arnold Lunn, Sir Henry's eldest son and brother of Hugh Kingsmill, later one of my closest friends.

Alec Vidler had already completed his degree course at Selwyn College, Cambridge, when I went up. That he, a

fourth-year man, should take an interest in a Freshman was in itself a surprise to me, and a fascination. Alec had already decided on his vocation; and he showed me that the Church was not 'silly' – which was the view that obtained in our Fabian household. He joined a caring Order, the Order of the Good Shepherd, with which indeed I chose to live myself during my last term at Cambridge. From Cambridge he then moved on to Birmingham, and later to St George's Chapel, Windsor, as assistant to the Canon.

Alec was an Anglo-Catholic. If he had been a Catholic he would have belonged to an Order which had a longer tradition and a more solid foundation. As it was, he was never put in charge of a parish although his very special quality of sanctity would undoubtedly have made him an excellent priest-in-charge. Instead, and also because he was in personal terms unambitious, he gravitated towards academic life. He became first Warden of Hawarden, Gladstone's old home where he had left a large library. Next he became editor of the magazine *Theology*, an important post but, according to Alec himself, 'un-exciting'. From there he went on to be Dean at King's College, Cambridge where among other things he was responsible for initiating the famous Carol Service. He never married because, on joining the Order of the Good Shepherd, he took a vow never to do so, and Alec is a man of his word, even though the Order broke up in a formal sense and many of its other members did marry.

He used to take a considerable part in College missions, and in missions such as those to the hop-pickers; but in discussing his own opinions and predilections he is a reticent man, modest and scholarly. I have also wondered occasionally if he was something of a disappointed man, for he does not seem to have achieved openly the success and influence to which his ability should entitle him. But to watch him cooking a meal for his guests in his house in Rye – the oldest in the town of which he was the last undistrictized mayor – is to forget any such thought in the warmth of his welcome, of his humanity and width of reference. He has been a lifetime's friend to me; and I hope that I have been as good and as lasting a friend to him.

At Alwaye, myself with two colleagues on the teaching staff.

In my fourth year at Cambridge I met Rev. W.E.S. Holland of the Church Missionary Society. He invited me to go out to South India and teach English Literature at the new Union Christian College at Alwaye, which was affiliated to the University of Madras. I accepted. It was a spur-of-the-moment decision, typical of most of the important decisions I have had to make in my life.

The Church of South India in Travancore (now Kerala) was the first to amalgamate with other churches, bringing together the Anglicans, the Syrian Christian Church (said to have been founded by St Thomas the apostle), and even some Catholics from the Portuguese areas.

At the College I was provided with my own servant, Kuruvella. The students, I found, had their own peculiar ways of learning, one of which was to commit lectures to memory. What worried me was that they often memorized even the bad lectures.

'Indian education,' Macaulay had decreed when he was a member of the supreme council of India from 1834 to 1838, 'should be in English.' Passing exams, therefore, was never easy for an Indian student. Indians are, however, exceedingly intelligent and resourceful, and this certainly proved to be the case when they needed to find out what the exam questions were going to be. The question papers were printed on a flat-bed press. One of the students, wearing the characteristic long white shirt called a mundu (worn as trousers in the rest of India), lay on the type. The impression was blurred and uneven, but legible.

One of the distinctive groups in South India was the Niars. They were not Christians, and all authority and all lines of inheritance lay in the hands of the women. This 'female power' made for the happiest, most charming, most carefree group of men I have ever come across.

When Gandhi visited the College he came alone, by train, in a third-class carriage and wearing only a loincloth. The crowds were waiting at the station. Immediately he arrived he walked across to one group who were cordonned off from the rest. They were the 'Untouchables'. His greeting them in this way was a great gesture on his part, and one that was genuinely felt.

The students and staff of Union Christian College, Rev. W.E.S. Holland centre, myself second from left, front row.

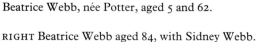
Beatrice Webb, née Potter, aged 5 and 62.

RIGHT Beatrice Webb aged 84, with Sidney Webb.

In 1927, I returned to England and was reunited with Kitty Dobbs. I went to Birmingham to work as a supply teacher, and it was there that we were married. The only member of Kitty's family who was present was her father, George Dobbs. Just before we signed the register, he called out, 'You can still get away, Kit!' Kitty's famous aunt, Beatrice Webb, did not attend, even though the ceremony was not in church but in a register office.

I sometimes used to feel that marrying Kitty Dobbs was like marrying into the Fabian royal family. Beatrice Webb, that formidable lady, and her husband Sidney were pioneer figures of the Fabian Society, and my father and his friends had always spoken of them with reverence. My father continued to do so, though with a

Kitty Muggeridge alongside a portrait of her mother, Beatrice's sister.

touch more acerbity when he heard her comment about him: 'A Fabian and a very worthy member of the Labour Party though of modest means.' ('To think,' my father remarked, 'that I gave up my directorship!')

The Webbs' own marriage, an arranged one, was certainly a marriage of minds, but of little else. Sidney was an absurd-looking little man with tiny legs and feet, a protruding stomach and a large head. He once sent his photograph to Beatrice. She returned it: 'I did not marry your body,' she wrote, 'I married your mind.' Of Bernard Shaw she told me: 'The first time I was alone with him he simply *threw* himself at me.' In her time she had nourished a passion for Joseph Chamberlain, but what particularly struck me about her was her beauty – a beauty of bone rather than of flesh, and extraordinarily reminiscent of Kitty. (See the photograph opposite of Kitty against the portrait of her own mother, Beatrice's sister.) Since in life you cannot have both love and power, Beatrice had clearly settled for power. Personally I think she would have been happiest as the Mother Superior of a Religious Order.

When, later, I went to Russia she assured me that 'Sidney and I are ikons in the Soviet Union'. Unfortunately I was to discover that even ikons have feet of clay. Kitty's own view of the Webbs was that they were humbugs: 'They always prided themselves on not owning a car, but they never stinted themselves on taxis. Perhaps they thought they were giving employment?!'

George Dobbs pointed out to me an Egyptian Government advertisement seeking teachers to teach English in Arab schools. As a result Kitty and I now travelled to Minia in Upper Egypt.

I later moved to the new Egyptian University of Cairo where the education was mostly in English and I had to lecture on set books in English literature. The students, however, were usually either away on strike helping the National Movement, the WAFD, or stupefying themselves with hashish. That was one reason why they struck me as much less intelligent than the Indian students.

Egyptian officials, among whom we teachers were numbered, wore the tarboosh; any Egyptian therefore who wanted to avoid trouble put on a hat (hawaga) instead of the tarboosh, for the tarboosh indicated loyalty to the 'dummy' ruler, installed by the British, King Fuad. He, poor fellow, used to bark when he spoke, having been shot in the neck. We were warned at the court that it was 'bad form' to notice the barking.

I remember our taking part in W.B. Yeats's unperformable verse play, *Countess Kathleen*. But the lines defeated us. One of Kitty's was 'The path is overgrown with thickets now.' I played an angel. 'The light beats down,' the angel proclaimed.

In Cairo I began writing articles about Egypt and its politics, cotton, even the use of English; and I met the special correspondent of the *Manchester Guardian*, Arthur Ransome. Since he did not wish to continue reporting he encouraged me to submit my pieces to the paper, who accepted them and then invited me by cable to join the paper. I jumped at the chance.

Arthur Ransome was very good to me, both in Egypt and later in Manchester. He was just like a grown-up child, and had no reaction to or understanding of politics.

OPPOSITE ABOVE One of Kitty's and my favourite pastimes in Cairo was playing chess, which we usually did on the balcony.

OPPOSITE BELOW On one holiday Kitty and I, with Bryn Davis, travelled as deck passengers, with no cabin, from Cairo to Venice and back.

Arthur Ransome in Cairo, 1930, by Hilda Trefusis.

He originally went to Russia mainly to collect Russian children's books, and he stayed, one might say, for 'the greatest fairy tale of them all' – the Russian Revolution. He married a burly Russian woman, a secretary to Trotsky. His phenomenal success as a children's writer came after he gave up journalism. He belongs to that curious group of men, like J.M. Barrie or A.A. Milne, who mostly had no children of their own, usually disliked children anyway, and yet had an astonishing gift for communicating with them. – But why is it easier to admire authors whom one does not know?

I was overjoyed at becoming a journalist on the *Manchester Guardian*. It was the next best thing to becoming a writer, and this was an ambition that had already formed in my mind. Also, the *Guardian* was *the* paper sacred to leftists, and especially to a family like ours which had eaten and drunk politics with every meal. So in 1930 Kitty and I packed our bags again and travelled to Manchester where I became a leader writer at a salary of £5 per week, which was adequate then for two adults, one child and a car!

The great father figure and editor of the *Manchester Guardian* was C.P. Scott. He, and the paper, were the last great voice of liberalism. I joined it at the height of the Depression, but if there was any depression at the paper it was because C.P. himself continued to edit it – and to demand to see everything that came in or was written – even though he had retired and the official editor was his son Ted Scott. For me this was a period not only of learning about journalism, on the hoof as it were; it also gave me my first taste of liberal humbug.

C.P. Scott had an endearing habit of writing a polite note should a piece he had commissioned not be used. Once I had had to write a short leader on a new gasometer built in Manchester, but it did not appear because of a special feature in the paper. C.P. wrote: 'There are occasions when it is necessary to economize truth in order not to make a hard task harder.' Inimitable, pure liberalism.

Precisely because the paper was sacred to leftists, it seemed a great betrayal when it supported the National Government of Ramsay, or 'Ramshackle', MacDonald. By then C.P. had died and I had been urging Ted Scott not to follow the National tide; but after Ted's sad drowning it was the new editor W.P. Crozier's views that prevailed.

Meanwhile, however, I applied for a post in Moscow. As far as I was concerned the capitalist system – with or without liberal pretensions – was breaking down. Did Russia offer an alternative?

I arrived in Moscow on 16 September 1932. The paper's regular correspondent, William Henry Chamberlin, was due to go on leave. His primary allegiance was to the *Christian Science Monitor*, and he would temper his views from one newspaper to the other – so that,

C.P. Scott.

'FIVE YEAR PLAN DOING WELL' meant, according to his Russian wife Sonia, that 'He is thinking of me'. Chamberlin would be less stern in his criticisms of Russia in the *Manchester Guardian* because, apart from the proclivities of the two newspapers, that would also enable him to write more frankly in the *Christian Science Monitor*.

In October 1932 the Soviet Government took all the foreign correspondents in Moscow to see a new dam and power-station. I wrote in my diary: 'Jogging along the lovely rolling Ukraine, we dingy cargo of seedy intellec-

Western journalists on journey to Dnieper-Stroi. Sonia Chamberlin is in front of me. Her husband was on leave.

tuals, "chauvinist" socialists, and down-at-heel journalists were carried to Dnieper-Stroi alternately stuffing ourselves with food, chattering together, and sleeping.' This trip, which gave most of us our first sight of the Russia of peasants and workers, was an eye-opener which depressed one English leftist whose enthusiasm for Communism diminished after finding himself among underfed and deprived peasants. This event, followed some months later by my own visit to the famine areas of the Ukraine, convinced me that the Russian experiment was not working. 'You cannot make people good through power, although you can through love.' However much the Russian intelligentsia bowed its head to Stalin, Russia was not proving to be an earthly paradise, except perhaps to the American colonel who had been in charge of building the dam. 'How do you like it here?' I asked somewhat banally. 'Wonderful,' he replied. 'We never have any labour troubles!'

I wrote a series of articles about the famine for the *Manchester Guardian* and sent them home by diplomatic bag. But I knew that as soon as they were published – and they were, although quite severely toned down by Crozier – I would become *persona non grata* in the Soviet Union, and expelled. This is precisely what happened.

Myself in Cairo in 1928 (left), and in Montreux in 1933. Do my experiences in Russia show?

From Moscow I went to Switzerland, where Kitty rejoined me, and there I wrote my novel *Winter in Moscow* which was published that same year, 1933. My publisher, Douglas Jerrold, welcomed it wholeheartedly: 'The Truth at last!' he claimed.

In Switzerland I was able to do some work for the League of Nations. The International Labour Office in Geneva was trying to gather information about disarmament from every country. As the replies came in we found that they were either spurious or the information was 'not available'. This was scarcely surprising since by its nature the information had to come from the interested governments.

The League, sadly, was apt to succumb to such flights of fantasy. As a result dismay and disillusion with its work, its activities and even its aims grew until a final ironic twist brought the end of so much idealism (is idealism in politics always misplaced?). On the day Germany invaded Poland in 1939, the League was discussing the unifying of the level-crossing systems throughout Europe. Which, I suppose, would have made invasion even easier!

When I came back to England from Geneva I found it impossible to get a job on Fleet Street. My reports from Russia, and *Winter in Moscow*, had dismayed the liberal consensus which still looked upon the Communist 'experiment' with a tolerant eye. When *The Times* turned me down I realized that I would have to search further afield – and this brought me back to India as a deputy editor on the Calcutta *Statesman*.

It was a very different India in 1934 compared to ten years previously. The white man's position in the Raj was beginning to become uncertain and this was mirrored in the *Statesman*. It was staffed entirely by whites; its view was liberal but naturally – and in support of the 'box-wallah' or business community, who were mainly in jute – it assumed the continuance of the Raj together with some enlightened cant on handing over in the future to (English)-educated Indians. So its style was often bland and, as articles were unsigned, I found, many years later – when James Cameron and I were reading through its files – that I could not identify what I had written.

The Englishman's home from home was the Bengal Club whose members were only white. It was possible to entertain Indians there but it had to be done in a private room. With the Nationalist Movement growing strongly, the club was increasingly becoming the Englishman's castle too.

The result was that, when I made friends with a group of Indians, we normally met in their homes or in restaurants. Even Shahid Suhrawardy, Professor of Fine Arts at the University of Calcutta, could not be elected to the Bengal Club. Nor could Chanda, Director of Education for Bengal, let alone Goswami, a Nationalist and Congressman, and a very rich landowner. Nor Sudhin Datta, poet, editor and previously secretary to Rabindranath Tagore, the one of the four of whom I was fondest.

One incident in Calcutta should have brought home to me something of the nature of both the Raj and the country. A car in which I was travelling knocked over an Indian in the street. To avoid the crowd that inevitably collected, we picked him up and took him to hospital. There I was appalled by what I saw. Someone had even cut his own throat. Squalor and dereliction, human and material, were everywhere. As a member of the Raj, even a minor one, I was viewing all this from, so to speak, a position of comfort. Nearly forty years later I discussed this with Mother Teresa and compared my reaction, which was to do nothing, with her response, which was to undertake the sort of practical action which has aroused the feelings and admiration of the whole world. (See page 96.)

Sudhin Datta whom I regularly used to meet in Calcutta.

Myself with Amrita Sher-Gil in Simla, with her Hungarian mother
and her Sikh father, a landowner and a disciple of Tolstoy.

32

The editor of the *Statesman*, Arthur Moore, supported the Raj in the same 'enlightened' way as his paper, so that he tended to regard me as 'bolshy'. He sent me to Simla – the intimate town in the hills north of Delhi to which the government went in summer – where there were no motor cars, only rickshaws, but where one could meet influential people and get a close view of government. The Raj was described by the Viceroy, Willingdon – a nice man but inevitably a comic-opera figure – as 'the easiest country in the world to govern'. Protocol was sedulously observed, however; and the only people who were lower in the pecking order than the journalists were the missionaries.

It was in Simla that I met a most remarkable young artist, Amrita Sher-Gil, part Indian, part Hungarian. I recall the physical intensity with which she worked, so different from the concentration of the writer whose effort is primarily intellectual. She had an enormous joy in the sensuality of the world, in animals, in colours – and this gave her painting its tremendous vitality. And herself too, for that matter. She is now recognized as one of the outstanding artists of modern India despite the fact that she died in 1941, only six years after I met her, when she was barely 29. A room in the Delhi Art Gallery is dedicated to her, and it includes the portrait she made of me in Simla.

While I was in Simla I received a telegram from Percy Cudlipp, the editor of the *Evening Standard* in London. He had seen some of my political articles and offered me a job which I promptly accepted, for it would not only bring me home but would at last gain me an entrée into Fleet Street. I flew home and was met by Kitty and her father at Croydon. We arranged to take a house in Grove Terrace, Kentish Town, near Parliament Hill Fields; and from there I was able to take the tram to work every day as far as Holborn.

The job turned out to be on the 'Londoner's Diary' gossip column where I wrote some two or three paragraphs a day. Lord Beaverbrook, the proprietor, who insisted on seeing all new recruits, gave me the recipe: 'Keep up the pretence that you move in High Society.'

This was not always too easy for someone without such pretensions, nor when news was lacking. A sovereign remedy for this was given me by one of the sub-editors. 'I can't see any promising subjects this morning,' I said

as I perused the other newspapers. He replied: 'Have you looked at the stiffs?' He was referring to the deaths column.

The people I saw most on the Diary were Randolph Churchill, Patrick (Lord) Kinross, and John Betjeman. Betjeman was Film Critic of the *Evening Standard* but used to contribute odd paragraphs. I knew him for many years, liked him, yet felt a sense of mystery about him.

John Betjeman.

Never did I meet any of his relations, nor do I recall anyone who did. There was in him too a certain coolness or standing-offness in personal relationships which can even be read into the famous poem about Miss J. Hunter Dunn. He also had a predisposition to melancholy, which led him often into practical joking. One of the more serious instances of this occurred when he met the Liberal Foreign Secretary, Sir John Simon, a severe, stuffed-shirt sort of character, on a London street. John Betjeman fell down in front of him, feigning an epileptic fit, which left the politician helpless and at sea, wondering what to do. Who would have thought then that Betjeman would become Poet Laureate?

Lord Beaverbrook had a peculiar habit, but not an unknown one among proprietors, of liking to pay his staff personally and in cash. Thus did I receive from his hand each week three crisp white five-pound notes.

Lord Beaverbrook's way of running his newspapers was interestingly different from how C.P. Scott ran the *Manchester Guardian*. Scott had views which, though I rarely found them sympathetic, were fairly consistent. Beaverbrook had no real views at all. What he had were moods, prejudices, sudden likes and dislikes. He might reverse a position he had held previously as the result of one conversation; or he might, after a row with one of his children, suddenly start a campaign for higher death duties. Hugh Kingsmill hit him off neatly when he called him 'Robin Badfellow'. He operated with money, and his journalists had somehow to respond to the prevailing wind. The trouble was, Beaverbrook believed his own newspapers even when he had fashioned them to put over his favourite fantasies – such as that there would be no war. Since war with Germany would clearly come eventually this attitude of unrelenting unreality affected all of us on the Diary – who were left merely to judge the state of Lord Beaverbrook's female connections from the nature of the copy sent down to us.

In 1937 this situation seemed to leave me with just one chance of making myself a writer before war supervened. So I packed the job in.

Lord Beaverbrook, 1926, by Low.

Randolph Churchill and I were together on the *Evening Standard* 'Londoner's Dairy' in 1936–7. Our friendship suffered during the *Punch* controversy over his father (1954, see page 63) but the estrangement did not last, I am glad to say, although he himself suffered in life sometimes from being rather like his father's ghost. This picture was taken in Downing Street in September 1940.

The family (now five of us) went to live in Sussex – at Whatlington, near Battle – where we bought a house for £800. There I settled down to write – first *The Thirties*, then a play. Previously I had had one play, *Three Flats*, performed by the Stage Society in London. Now my second was to be *Autumnal Face*. The *Daily Telegraph* gave me regular fiction reviewing.

Two people whom I saw a lot of at this time were Hugh Kingsmill, who lived nearby in Hastings, and Hesketh Pearson, already making a reputation as a biographer. We all enjoyed walking and talking, particularly Hughie who was one of those people who put their genius into their lives, but whose literary aspirations and products are seldom successful. He must have received unearned advances from most of the eminent London publishers but they were never grudged. He was a man of rare quality, very observant and very funny. Even nowadays, the better part of forty years since he died, he is seldom far from my happiest thoughts.

When the war duly came, I tried to join up but my age (36) was comparatively high and journalism was a reserved occupation (why?!). I did succeed, however, in finding a post with the Ministry of Information ('Ministry of Morale' as a book later called it) which was based mainly in the University of London buildings in Malet Street.

One of the hazards of life at this period was negotiating the London 'black-out'. With no street lights operating, the whores used to ply their wares on the pavements with the help of shaded bicycle lamps.

Perhaps because he produced the delightful 'CARELESS TALK COSTS LIVES' posters for the Ministry of Information, the phoney war period always makes me think of the figure of Kenneth Bird, or 'Fougasse'. These posters have become collectors' items. Bird took the name Fougasse from a French bomb which blew him up during the First World War. He then had completely to relearn how to draw. He became a Christian Scientist, and editor of *Punch*, and I was to see a lot of him when I joined the magazine in the 1950s. He was particularly clever at the 'ordinary man' cartoon. In one series the quiet man leaves home for work in the City in the morning only to return in the evening, after a day's business, behaving like a maniac.

At the 'height' of the phoney war I wrote an article for the *Daily Telegraph* in which I indicated that 'this is an extraordinary war because it is so difficult to get into the army'. The paper printed a letter written in reply: 'If you are not bluffing, come and join the Field Security Police. We need linguists and have been advertising for some time.'

So now I found myself a private, in breeches and puttees, at Mytchett Hutments in Surrey, not far from Aldershot, being drilled by the CMPs (Corps of Military Police). I was ambitious to get into Operations, and as I was also the only person on the course with press experience, I was to lecture on 'handling the press'. Then I was made a sergeant and sent on an Intelligence course.

Military wedding group, 1940, myself as sergeant extreme left.

One of the faces I met during the Intelligence course had the Nietzsche-like 'soup-strainer' moustache of Enoch Powell. At first he did not look like a natural soldier, but when he started putting some shrewd questions to me I realized he was the most intelligent man on the course. Later in the war, when he was a brigadier in Cairo, he took what must surely be unique action in resigning his post in protest at what he saw as the Allies' failure to take advantage of the collapse of the Italian government in 1943. He wanted us to invade Northern Italy and reach Vienna and Prague before the Russians. At the time it was scarcely a practical policy although, as usual with Enoch, there was hard and realistic thinking behind it. One wonders what was MI6's view?

Enoch was sent to India where he became infatuated with the Raj and wanted to ensure its continuance after the war. He became Tory MP for Wolverhampton and a member of the Conservative Research Department. Most politicians do not believe what they say but Enoch, essentially a fundamentalist, really does. It is what informs his earnest, hypnotic eloquence.

After the Intelligence course I was posted, with a commission, to Sheerness where we were the only military force available to repel any invasion. But the invasion, when it occurred, was not the feared German one but French, as thousands of dispirited troops arrived from across the Channel with their often antique guns and side-arms. I did my best to encourage them to join the Free French but they mostly seemed apathetic. 'And now,' I used to say in last resort, 'let us pray for France and see what that will do.'

Soon after this I managed to get a posting to GHQ, Home Forces, first at Kneller Hall (where they normally train military bandsmen), then at St Paul's School in Hammersmith. At our billet nearby in Edith Road a fellow officer chose to ignore the washing facilities of the house and use camp equipment in his own room. I discovered later that this enabled him to claim field allowance in addition to his pay.

Here I met again Bobby Barclay who had been at Mytchett. He was the step-son of Sir Robert (later Lord) Vansittart of the Foreign Office. One day my CO asked me to investigate a house in Holland Park whose

Enoch Powell, photographed ten years after the war, by which time he was in government. We met in the war; in the 1970s we debated in St Mary-le-Bow (see page 87).

occupants were believed to have dubious political associations, i.e. with Fascism. The reason for investigating was that the Commander-in-Chief, General Ironside, appeared frequently to be visiting the house and he was known to have such affiliations. It turned out that his visits were of a personal nature, not political, but they were more frequent than seemed right for a C-in-C in wartime.

Embarrassed myself, and not wishing to embarrass my CO, I consulted with Bobby and we agreed to go straight to Vansittart. Vansittart heard us without batting an eyelid, impassively, even. We bought an evening paper later on, the headline of which said 'IRONSIDE SACKED'. Bobby and I felt terrible, shattered. On reflection, however, I realized that, at most, our report had simply confirmed action already decided upon.

From GHQ, Home Forces, I was despatched to 5 Corps in Longford Castle near Salisbury. There I was given an office labelled 'Security Intelligence' and the title of Intelligence Officer. My first impression was of the notices that were displayed all over the camp which said 'ARE YOU FULL OF BINGE?' Binge? I asked myself.

Monty, close to the time I first knew him. Here, as a Lieutenant-General and the newly appointed Commander-in-Chief of Southern Command, he is about to inspect the young soldiers battalion in December 1941.

When I joined 5 Corps as a captain I was made Intelligence Officer. I always tried to look urgent, but this does not seem to be one of those moments.

This turned out to be my first acquaintance with a man whom, after the war, I grew to know quite well – Major-General (as he then was) Sir Bernard Montgomery, or 'Monty'. It was a perfect example of his prep school type of ebullience, complete to the misuse of the word 'binge'. But even then he seemed to be the right man in the right place at the right time. I recall a splendid pep talk he once gave to the Sanitary Unit – 'you cannot imagine what damage you can do to the enemy with a properly aimed hose!'

After the war, when Montgomery was offered the job of C-in-C, Malaya – with the special task of cracking down on the Communist insurrection – he opted instead to stay on as NATO Deputy Supreme Commander in the Château at Fontainebleau in the hope, eventually, of being made C-in-C, Home Forces. Did he harbour a hope of being called on to settle the troubles at home like a dictator? However that may be, the Malaya job was given to General Templer, who made a success of it, and Monty resented him for it.

Montgomery's ego was ever in the ascendant. He always felt himself to be religious (he was the son of a bishop) and he was very sparing with casualties, one of the most cautious of generals. This was a reason why he was also one of the most successful.

After some months at 5 Corps, and unsuccessfully trying to transfer to a combat unit, I received a mysterious order to present myself at an address in London to be considered for special Intelligence duties. Some time before this Grahame Greene and I had concocted a scheme through his sister Liza who worked in MI6. I was accepted, but my transfer to MI6 proved to be a wonderfully convoluted affair.

Apparently one could not just be posted. I had to appear to be a civilian and, to fortify this impression, I was given a passport stamped to indicate that I had just landed in the UK. I now needed to be issued with a civilian ration book and identity card. 'Tell them,' I was instructed before I entered Caxton Hall where these vital matters were attended to, 'tell them you have just come from the United States, and that you will be doing some more travelling ere long.' I objected that this was not true, and what would I say if I were questioned? Of course, I wasn't asked anything, and my story, full of its obvious pitfalls, was accepted, but I did start asking myself why it is that the Secret Service does not really feel it is doing its job properly unless it is creating a sense of mystery and fantasy.

The intention, we gathered, was to open up various new stations in Africa. Graham Greene was to go to Freetown, I to Lourenço Marques in Mozambique. I repaired to *Encyclopaedia Britannica* to bolster my knowledge of that country to help me fulfil my assigned role as a British Vice-Consul.

After two years of the London black-out Lisbon, when we landed there by night, seemed like a celestial vision, but the long delay, and then the journey to Lourenço Marques via Madeira, Lobito, Elizabethville and Nairobi made me think wistfully that, if I had decided to stay in Portugal, no one could have stopped me! Once in Lourenço Marques, however, there was enough to do and think about. I was responsible to an immediate superior in Kenya but my ultimate boss in MI6 was a man called Philby.

One day when I was driving a car in Mozambique, I lost control of the steering. My suspicion that it had been tampered with was reinforced by the fact that ever afterwards the Italian Consul refused to look me in the face. Only in the fantasy world of espionage could he ever have imagined that encompassing my death could contribute to the winning of the war by the Axis powers.

OPPOSITE My document of appointment as British Vice-Consul at Lourenço Marques, 1942, signed by the Consul, Claude Ledger. The signal to Berlin at the time from the German Consul stated that I was in charge of all espionage activities on the eastern coast of Africa.

By me, Claude Kirwood Ledger, Esquire,
His Britannic Majesty's Acting Consul General
residing at Lourenço Marques.

Be it known to all to whom these presents
shall come that, by virtue of the powers vested in
me by His Majesty's Commission, I do hereby consti-
tute and appoint Mr. Thomas Malcolm MUGGERIDGE to be
British Vice-Consul at Lourenço Marques with full
power and authority, by all lawful means, to aid and
protect His Majesty's subjects trading in, visiting
or residing in his district.

Witness my hand and seal of office at
Lourenço Marques, this twenty-ninth day
of June, 1942.

C. K. Ledger.

Authority:-

Telegram from Foreign Office
Nº 24 dated 8th March, 1942.

Lourenço Marques was, of course, a neutral port. One of the uses of a neutral port to the belligerents was as a place where enemies could meet and do business. In one case a Swedish ship was carrying out an exchange of diplomats between Britain and Japan. There was also a number of Jews being repatriated from China, the one country, I believe, where they have never become assimilated. I met the Swedish captain in the ideal place for doing business – a bordello. Inevitably, there were MI6 people in both exchange parties. The picture shows the British ambassador in Japan telling the British Consulate staff what happened to him there. The poor fellow doesn't seem to be arousing much interest or belief.

As a vice-consul I dealt with the communication of

information to the home country and tried to interrupt the flow of news to Berlin. In fact Wertz, the German Consul, was so worried by our activities – helped by the code-breaking at Bletchley – that the passage of information to his superiors was made considerably more difficult. We used to meet, since we lived in the same hotel, but we never did more than bow formally to each other and proceed on our different ways. Wertz was later sent as ambassador to Lisbon, and retired to Munich after the war.

Some years later I heard that he had fallen from a bridge in Munich and been killed. The news reached me, curiously, via the German Consul in Liverpool because in some way my name had emerged from Wertz's files. I wrote a letter of sympathy to his widow, but heard no more. There was never any question, however, of Wertz tampering with the steering of my car.

Graham Greene is almost the same age as I am. I have always been very fond of him, for he is a kind and generous man who helps people in a quiet, unobtrusive and practical way. And our experiences in Intelligence in Africa in the Second World War were nearly parallel.

He is one of England's finest storytellers and novelists. At present his fame stands very high, certainly because of his sheer craftsmanship, ability to entertain at a serious level and his sense of irony, but possibly also, I wonder, because this is a comparatively lean period in this country for literature. I even sometimes suspect that future generations might see him as lightweight and see us as lacking in seriousness, too, for holding him in such high regard, particularly over his later novels.

There is a hint of something almost perverse and quixotic about him at times – witness his 'championing' of Kim Philby, our MI6 boss! When Philby intrigued against his chief at MI6, a man who had been imported from the Indian Civil Service, Graham was outraged, and resigned. Yet he will profess amusement at the idea of Philby, the Russian plant, taking over the Secret Service. Perhaps there is a mischievous boy in all of us who delights in such adventurous ironies for their own sake?

Graham Greene photographed in 1954.

In 1943 I was given a new assignment in Algeria, which led the following year to my being sent to Paris to work in co-operation with the French Securité Militaire. My superior now was Victor Rothschild who requisitioned as our headquarters the Rothschild mansion on the Boulevard Suchet. Usefully it had a very large back door, and under the Occupation it had been the residence of General Wedemeyer. What was remarkable, though, was that neither in 1940 nor in 1944 was it looted by the Germans even though it was known to be a Jewish house. Everything, even the valuable pictures on the walls, had been left undisturbed. My French colleague M. Felix summed up the reasons: 'Hitlers come and go, but Rothschilds go on for ever'.

The Liberation of Paris in 1944 by the Allied Forces was a tumultuous occasion; but it was also a very ugly scene indeed, and frequently sad.

I was in Paris quite early on. At this stage the scene was not only ugly, but confused as well; and the politicians, suffering from a greater or lesser sense of guilt according to the degree to which they had collaborated with the Germans, were even more confused.

My view was that, if a country is taken over by an enemy you either collaborate up to a point or you leave. Therefore it was wrong, I felt, to shave heads – which was frequently done to 'collaborators' of minor degree, particularly girls who had slept with German soldiers billeted in their houses. Of course there was no proper authority at this time; and many people denounced others in order to demonstrate their own innocence or protect their own guilt. The prison at Frennes included people – particularly politicians, actors, restaurateurs and prostitutes – who had simply entertained Germans. But arrests went on at a high level too, publicly supported by the newspapers which dramatized the whole scene in hysterical style, the most infamous case being that of Pierre Laval whose trial turned into a public purging of the nation's guilt.

The whole situation made such a deep and lasting impression upon me that I later wrote a play called *Liberation*. But it created one genuine hero – Charles de Gaulle.

Ironically the Allies wanted to keep General de Gaulle, who had of course been the leader of the Free French forces in London from 1940–4, out of France until elections were held. But de Gaulle disdained such

advice; he simply walked in and took over.

I always think of de Gaulle as symbolized in the incident at the cathedral of Notre Dame. By some mistake, during the Thanksgiving service for Liberation, a

44

Winston Churchill and General de Gaulle in Paris in 1944. I cannot help feeling that together they look like Don Quixote and Sancho Panza; but neither of them, I suspect, would have seen the joke. They were uneasy allies.

But for him, the communists – very strong in the Resistance – would have taken over power in Paris and throughout the country. Without him no durable regime would have been created. He was a most extraordinary, *the* most extraordinary, political leader I have experienced – distinguished, stylish, regal – of exceptional intelligence, dominant of course, but never hysterical. Inside him too there lurked a weird, personal sense of comedy.

I recall two occasions in particular. The first concerns his able lieutenant Jacques Soustelle whom de Gaulle later appointed Governor-General of Algeria and who told me this story himself. Although he was of the Left, Soustelle had sympathy for the Algerian French. At the time that led up to the Algerian war, Soustelle reported to de Gaulle: 'All my friends deplore your policies.' De Gaulle replied: 'Alors, mon vieux, changez vos amis.'

The second occasion concerns de Gaulle's daughter. She was much loved and cherished by her father who devoted himself to her whenever he could. She was mongoloid and, as most such are, a very loving and affectionate person. When she died at twenty-one, he gave a brief, dignified, deeply moving homily over her grave: 'Maintenant elle est comme les autres.' – 'Now she is just like everyone else.'

One way in which de Gaulle's lurking sense of humour showed itself was on a day when he was inspecting a parade. He stopped suddenly in front of a coloured soldier. 'Vous êtes nègre,' he said. 'Oui, mon Général, je suis nègre,' came the reply. 'Alors, continuez.' ('Carry on.').

On his retirement in 1970 he went to Ireland for a much publicized holiday and rest. I wrote to him then, reminded him that his first famous broadcast in 1940 had been from the BBC. Why not now end the same way?

I received the following reply from him – magisterial as ever but with that strange humour I had often observed, especially in the way he refers to broadcasting as 'the waves': 'Je n'envisage pas d'utiliser les ondes' (see over).

pistol was fired. The whole congregation fell flat to the floor – except for one man. De Gaulle himself, aloof, absolute, was the only person who remained upright, like a lamp-post.

LEFT AND BELOW Myself in Paris, 1944.

le 19 Fevrier 1970

Monsieur,

Veuillez être assuré que je n'oublie pas la B.B.C. et le précieux appui que j'y ai souvent trouvé dans l'accomplissement de ma mission pendant la guerre.

Ce souvenir et les très aimables sentiments exprimés dans votre lettre m'étaient autant de motifs de la considérer avec intérêt.

Mais je n'envisage pas d'utiliser les ondes dorénavant ou d'y fair diffuser aucun message et ne puis, de ce fait, donner suite à l'offre que vous avez bien voulu me soumettre et dont je vous remercie.

Veuillez croire, Monsieur, à mes sentiments les plus distingués et les meilleurs.

(sgd) C. de Gaulle

Monsieur Malcolm Muggeridge,
Room 2066,
Kensington House,
Richmond Way,
LONDRES 14, Grande-Bretagne.

The French government was very grateful for the work
of British Intelligence in the liberation of France and of
Paris, and it expressed this in many awards. For my part
I deeply appreciate the 'Médaille de la Reconnaissance
Française', accorded me by de Gaulle, my 'Chevalier de
la Légion d'Honneur', and my Croix de Guerre.

One of the tasks that had been deputed to me in Paris was to 'look after' P.G. ('Plum') and Ethel Wodehouse. The problem was to keep him out of England when the French police were anxious to send him to London. If he had gone to London it is probable he would have been arrested, tried and condemned like William Joyce (Lord Haw-Haw) and John Amery; and all because of innocuous broadcasts he had given in Berlin in 1939–40 for which, as he put it, he had only been given 'the statutory fee'.

'What do you think about all this?' I asked him.

'Like being a comedian and you go on stage and you get the bird,' he replied.

The Germans, of course, believed that the picture of the English gentleman as given in Wodehouse's novels was correct. If so, he could be said to have provided the evidence that trapped many spies!

The French police were prepared to release Wode-house, but only so long as he was certified as being 'ill'. They were happy, indeed relieved, first to liberate Ethel and her Pekinese dog 'Wonder'. 'Plum' himself was then released into a maternity home, because proper hospital accommodation was short; after which the three of them went to live in a Fontainebleau hotel and I went to London to try and get for him some of his accrued royalties. His agents very properly did not reveal the state of his earnings beyond saying that his highest royalties came, of all places, from Japan, with whom, of course, we were still at war.

'What do you think about religion?' I asked Plum one day. 'Not really,' he answered. He did not live in this world, of course, and so he preserved an astonishing and endearing innocence. 'Life is absurd, but also wonderful,' seemed to sum it all up for him. He did add, however, 'The cads have taken over.' He never returned to England.

To Malcolm and Kitty
with love from
Plummie and Ethel.

When the time came for me to leave the army, I acted as if in a dream. I simply put on a civilian suit and went home – to Kitty and the family in Whatlington. In Intelligence, even one's demobilization is secret!

But my difficulties did not end just like that. One of the policies of MI6 was never to divulge salaries (though mine, as a major's, could have been guessed) for in part they were paid tax-free. At one stage I found I was being paid two salaries, but earning one.

I joined the *Daily Telegraph*. It was a good job, really quite interesting, but after I had found my feet the daily offering of ideas for editorials, and writing them, began to pall. We were not free to take our own decisions, and even the editor, Arthur Watson, had to refer upstairs – to Lord Camrose and his family on the fifth floor. After about ten months I heard that the paper's Washington correspondent was ending his term. I applied, got the job, and travelled over, as was normal then, by boat.

Lord Camrose, owner of the *Daily Telegraph*, at the paper in 1941.

Walking the deck, on the voyage to New York.

Photograph of Kitty Muggeridge taken during the war.

FROM THE NINETEEN-FORTIES
TO THE NINETEEN-EIGHTIES

The journalist's essential equipment of passports, visas, and passes reminds me of lines from *The Book of Job*: 'And the Lord said unto Satan, Whence comest thou? Then Satan answered the Lord, and said, From going to and fro in the earth, and from walking up and down in it.' (*Job*, 1:7)

So here I was in Washington, early in 1946, attending press conferences in the Oval Office of the White House. Since the 'S' in Harry S. Truman, as in Ulysses S. Grant, was only for euphony, the President had become known as 'Harry S for Nothing Truman'.

Truman was undistinguished but the embodiment of common sense. Perhaps his finest hour came when Israel was being formed. The Soviet Union and the United States were falling over themselves to recognize the new state. Arab journalists, and others, questioned the haste and protested. In a rare piece of honesty in a politician Truman responded, 'If you can tell me where else I can get votes in New York State I would drop the whole thing!' This unattributable remark was, of course, honoured; but after microphones were brought into Presidential news conferences, let alone cameras, less frankness and more fantasy crept into the reporting. 'The more open the diplomacy,' as someone said, 'the less open the diplomacy.' And that fantasy element in news reporting has increased ever since in direct proportion to the technical ability to spread the news.

President Truman, a 'small man' who grew in stature over the years and who was remarkably frank even in press conferences. This picture shows him in 1956, not much changed, resilient as ever.

At this time, not long after the end of the war, the United States was richer and looked like being more powerful than the whole of the rest of the world. It could have done anything it chose. But US leaders had no idea what to do, except to give their wealth away in such schemes as the Marshall Aid plan. They did not even think, for example, of trying to stabilize Latin America, let alone of Bertrand Russell's plan for a preventive war. The result was that the US became the mecca for everyone looking for a handout, be they countries, institutions or individuals. Even Molotov, the Russian Foreign Minister, applied, though his government quickly warned him off. Washington was besieged by crackpots, chisellers and genuine cases of every description.

It was a strange, muddled time. American naïveté was such that, before the end of the war, Roosevelt had given approval for the Russians to print US Occupation currency, and lent them the plates with which to do so. They became red-hot! But the mirror-image of that naïveté was America's immense generosity. No other country has ever been so generous. It was a period too of political muddle, in the run-up to the McCarthy era; to the Alger Hiss–Whittaker Chambers case; while we journalists were being briefed at the British Embassy by Donald Maclean who, at the time, was passing technical secrets to Russia.

I worked in an office within easy reach of the Senate and of the British Embassy in Massachusetts Avenue. Two tickertape machines worked twenty-four hours a day so that when I arrived each morning the office seemed submerged in yellow paper. I had little time for matters other than news-gathering and hardly ever even got outside Washington. All the stories seemed to be about money.

My paper kept on asking what the US intended to do. We did not know. The US government still did not know. And so the handout circus continued. But I did make one prediction which proved to be correct – that General Eisenhower, now ending his appointment as Chief of Staff, would run successfully for US President in 1952.

OPPOSITE I went to the US by boat across the Atlantic, but came back by air across the Pacific and via Japan.

54

I saw very little of America, indeed about the only time I got out of Washington was when I left it, and chose to go home the long way, via the Far East. Principally I wanted to see Japan and its current viceroy, General Douglas MacArthur, to whom I had an introduction from one of his fellow generals.

MacArthur received me smoking his cob pipe. The large, brooding presence which I had expected from wartime photographs was lessened by his being surprisingly short. He was also very vain, which the Japanese cleverly played upon by 'laying on' crowds to shout 'Banzai' whenever he appeared on the streets. He talked at me for nearly an hour. His theme was that the US Army had brought democracy and Christianity to the country and had thereby effected a revolution unique in history. 'Freedom is a heady wine,' he kept on saying, like a parody of the man of action.

I could not help thinking of the Emperor Hirohito. He had been told he was no longer to behave like a god, and should dress like a dapper civil servant, complete with homberg hat. But no one told him not to keep lifting it off and on, off and on, to acknowledge cheers. Like working a pump handle.

I went on to visit Hiroshima, to see for myself the devastation, the plans for rebuilding, and also whether the frequently-told horror stories were true. God knows the devastation was true; but I could not find evidence for the instantaneously fossilized hands or the bicycle melted into a bridge. Equally sceptical was a Jesuit who had been in Hiroshima when the bomb was dropped. I had no desire to diminish the horror or sense of outrage, however, which indeed was so great that it was already generating its own myths.

At a Foyle's Literary Luncheon with Mrs Randolph Churchill.

Back in London I resumed my former duties at the *Daily Telegraph*. There was a new editor, Colin Coote, but the atmosphere, and the fifth floor, were just the same. After three months I was once again finding leader writing infinitely wearisome. But at least I was covering a wider brief, such as the House of Commons. I was also finding it worthwhile to keep in touch with 'Monty', now Deputy Supreme Commander at SHAEF, who put me in the way of a number of inspired stories. I had, too, one memorable interview with Churchill at Westerham. He reminded me of King Lear, 'imprisoned in the

flesh, in old age, longing only for a renewal of the disease of life, all passion unspent', as I put it in my diary. Churchill was still out of power, of course, and he was seventy-five. So I could not think then that I might soon be angling for his resignation. I still had enormous affection and veneration for him.

Even though I was now Deputy Editor of the *Telegraph*, I was often finding life outside of greater interest and concern as I became increasingly involved in literary affairs – book reviewing, Arts programmes, advising publishers, editing the diaries of Count Ciano (Mussolini's foreign minister), even Literary Luncheons. It was also at this time that two of my closest literary friends died – Hughie Kingsmill and George Orwell.

When Hugh Kingsmill died in 1949 I and all his friends were greatly distressed. His character and charm were such that Hesketh Pearson and I decided to recall him in a book *About Kingsmill* which was based on letters we wrote to each other about him. This is part of what I wrote to Hesketh on 1 July 1949:

> You will agree with me that his genius found expression best in conversation with friends – the activity which, of all others, he found most pleasing, and for which he was invariably and wisely prepared to relinquish all other occupations. His books, especially his 'Johnson' and 'Frank Harris', are excellent, but, as you know, he found writing laborious. He wrote very slowly in that queer neat hand of his, adding up the words as he went along, usually in the Silence Room at the Authors' Club. I can see him there now so vividly, surrounded by books, and always ready to turn aside and talk. In conversation, ideas came flowing out of him in effortless profusion. I have never known anyone like him in this respect, and I doubt very much if there has ever been anyone quite like him. His talk ranged over everything, and illuminated everything. I dare say Johnson, whom he loved, was the same; but I doubt if even Johnson could produce quite the mingling of humour and insight, the, as it were, inexhaustible loving-kindness about life in all its manifestations which he could on all occasions.
>
> It was the first thing I noticed about him when we met in 1930. . . . He arrived [in Manchester] quite late on a Friday night, and we went to the station to meet him. You know that curious feeling one has of meeting someone with whom one is going to be intimate. You feel as though you know them already. Features, tone of voice, gestures, all are at once familiar. Thus I remember, in the dark, cavernous Manchester station with people streaming through the barrier, picking out Hughie without the slightest difficulty and greeting him as though we were old friends instead of strangers. He would have said that this was an example of reincarnation – an idea he was inclined to toy with.

My own view is that it is an instinctive recognition of some permanent aspect of life as distinct from its mere phenomena and sensations. People we are going to love we always have known, and will always know. There is never any novelty in what belongs to eternity.

If there ever was a modern physical embodiment of Don Quixote it was George Orwell. Like the Knight of the Woeful Countenance he was very lean and egotistic and honest and foolish – foolish in the sense that his attitudes were unreal because he combined extreme romanticism with a very dry interest in certain areas of life.

I remember P.G. Wodehouse saying that Orwell seemed a gloomy sort of chap. It is true that he gave this impression initially but, on closer acquaintance, he really was, in his own odd way, quite a happy man. But he was

obsessed, particularly in his need to expose the hypocrisy and chicanery of Communist policies. Hugh Kingsmill used to say that Orwell reminded him of a gate swinging on a rusty hinge.

When George died it was particularly sad because he was not ready to go, to relinquish life (he was only forty-six). He also had at least five books in him which he desperately wanted to write. At his funeral I found the sight of his coffin, so long because he was so tall, particularly poignant.

I often wonder what he, a very reticent and reserved man, although undoubtedly very emotional too, would have made of the '1984' celebrations in his honour. Everyone then seemed to be doing their Orwell piece. He would certainly have been very surprised, and very uncomfortable, at the praise and inquisitiveness visited upon him. On the other hand, he would have been gratified at the world-wide success and sales of *Animal Farm* and *1984*, for the former is a genuine modern classic and a frightening indictment of the pursuit of power through revolution, and he wrote the message to be heard.

In my opinion he was not a natural novelist, and he only seemed able to write sympathetically about humans when he was regarding them as 'animals', and even then the fiction was only a means to a non-fiction end. Yet he was a lovable man; and his vision of the collectivized state has an appalling veracity which will mean that the figures 1984 will always have two meanings.

Max Beerbohm was always marvellous and mellow company. In 1950 I visited him and his wife Florence in his house near Rapallo where he had lived ever since he left England. He was one of those people eminent in the Arts who left England for Europe when Oscar Wilde was arrested in 1895. With Hilaire Belloc he had tried to run a rival magazine to *Punch* called *Judy* for which he designed the cover himself.

In old age he spoke in a slightly tremulous way but with complete lucidity. Perhaps what was most remarkable about him then was that he had remained true to his own world and his own times and so had remained true to himself – even though by then a major new road had brought noisy traffic and its fumes very close to his beloved villa.

Sir Max Beerbohm, pictured in 1943.

A writer whom I ran into quite often at this time, and whose books I greatly admire, was Evelyn Waugh. I wrote in my diary in 1950: 'Quite ludicrous figure in dinner jacket and silk shirt . . . extraordinarily like a loquacious woman, with dinner jacket cut like a maternity gown to hide his bulging stomach. He was very genial, probably pretty plastered, and all the time playing this part of the crotchetty old character, rather deaf, cupping his ear – "fellow's a bit of a Socialist, I suspect". Amusing for about a quarter of an hour, then tedious.'

But this surface impression does not convey Waugh's inner quality or generosity of character which was expressed more privately and in a way that would help most.

Evelyn Waugh, photographed in 1955.

61

Man goeth forth unto his work and to his labour until the evening.

Late in 1952 I was approached by Christopher Chancellor, Head of Reuters. He told me *Punch* was seeking a new editor, a new broom. The magazine was, in fact, languishing. Its upper-middle-class and establishment character had not changed since before the war. Its cartoons of funny servants, comic schoolmasters, and its professed aim of making 'a little gentle fun about the garden mower', no longer seemed relevant even in dentists' waiting rooms. So I decided to accept the challenge.

I always felt that purely humorous magazines were not natural, so when I set about altering *Punch* (with the support of the management) I was not trying to remove the humour but to sharpen it, and to spice it with politics and current affairs. It was this approach and one special cartoon by Illingworth (opposite) that led us into trouble over the Prime Minister in the issue of 3 February 1954. This cartoon was certainly outspoken – in its open hint that Churchill should retire – but was it right? Or justified? A lot of people told me, in the controversy that followed, that we were right. But it also, temporarily at least, lost *Punch* readers, and myself a number of friends, including Randolph Churchill. But not for ever, I am glad to say.

What amazes me even now, however, is the reaction of Churchill himself, as it was reported by his doctor Lord Moran in the book *Churchill, Taken from the Diaries of Lord Moran* (1966). Moran himself was in Leeds when he was summoned on this occasion. As he arrived Churchill said, 'They have been attacking me. It isn't really a proper cartoon. The *Mirror* has had nothing so hostile. Look at my hands – I have beautiful hands.'

'*Punch* goes everywhere,' Churchill went on. 'I shall have to retire if this sort of thing goes on. I must make a speech in a fortnight's time,' he continued, 'it is necessary when things like this happen.'

It is understandable that Churchill should feel hurt. But how our most distinguished war leader and a veteran of the political scene from the early years of the century should worry about his hands and feel that he was 'finished' just because of one hostile cartoon in *Punch*, still baffles me.

'I've said it before, and I'll say it again – humour is a very serious business.'

The Editorial chair at *Punch*.

I did not know Augustus John (right) at all well, but we used to bump into each other at parties. He was an engaging ruffian, a good though perhaps not great painter, and he had a famous reputation with women. I said to him once, 'You've had an exciting life.' He replied, 'It's been terrible, terrible!' and he meant it.

Nor did I know Vicky, the cartoonist (far right), particularly well. He was never at home in England – somehow Club life in London could never compensate him for the loss of the café society of Berlin and its liveliness and gossip; but he was a marvellous draughtsman, and dominated the scene in the Macmillan era particularly. He had the great cartoonist's gift – anyone he drew, however caricatured, remained instantly recognizable.

In the photograph below Anthony Powell and Basil Boothroyd are on my left. On the other side are (left to right) Peter Dickinson, P.M. Hubbard (leaning on desk), Russell Brock, Leslie Marsh and B.A. Young.

In 1956 I joined the Anglo-Ukrainian Society in a vigorous protest at the official visit to Great Britain of Marshal Bulganin and Mr Khrushchev from the Soviet Union. In this photograph above are (left) Auberon Herbert, an old friend and Vice-Chairman of the Anglo-Ukrainian Society; Lady Hesketh; and Mick Wallwork, chairman of the protest we were staging at Coventry. It was public demonstrations and controversies such as this which tended to make the proprietors of *Punch* less keen to support me as editor, and me, in my turn, less keen on the limitations of an editorial chair. This was quite a tense time for me.

I was still at *Punch* in the late spring of 1957 when I spent a couple of weeks in America. It was then that the *Saturday Evening Post*, still a popular and influential magazine, commissioned an article from me on the theme of royalty and constitutional monarchy. They had seen an article of mine in the *New Statesman* called 'Royal Soap Opera' which had otherwise made very little impression. When my *Saturday Evening Post* piece eventually appeared (on 19 October 1957) I had left *Punch* and, unknown to me when I wrote it, the Queen was about to start on a tour of the US and Canada. If you read the article today you would wonder that there was ever any fuss, but fuss and controversy there certainly was (see the following pages). Part of the trouble was caused by the misleading title, not mine, which the magazine gave the article: 'Does England really need a Queen?'

It became a watershed in my working life.

Immediately news of the article broke, the BBC first invited me to defend it on *Panorama*, then banned me from television and broadcasting altogether. This made it very difficult for me to get other jobs. And it seemed to justify the action of one man in particular who spat in my face on the sea-front at Brighton. Even today, in the 1980s, there are people who decline to meet me because they believe I insulted the Queen.

I was invited to New York to discuss the article with Mike Wallace. The programme was screened, but not in Washington where it was blacked out to avoid offending the Royal party.

Amid the hysteria I have never forgotten the comfort and encouragement of one man's message to me: 'Never forget that only dead fish swim with the tide.'

And the lesson of it all? William Blake wrote, with peculiar appropriateness for television and for people who condemn others without reading what they have said:

> They ever must believe a lie
> Who see with, not through, the eye.

It was deeply unpleasant, although also valuable, to see how the Establishment can work; but what the imbroglio taught me was the humbling experience of anathema.

Leaving for New York on 19 October 1957, the day the *Saturday Post* article appeared.

Discussing it on television with Mike Wallace, 'the Rocky Marciano of Television'.

Back at our flat in Albany, thinking it all over.
Being anathema is a chastening experience.

Muggeridge: Fleet Street is dismayed

568

Sunday Express Correspondent
LONDON, Saturday.

Francis Williams, one of Britain's leading experts on the Press, writing in the Left-wing New Statesman, today declared he has found "surprise and dismay" in Fleet Street because th_ Dispatch appare_ hunt ag__

B.B.C. ban Muggeridge

B.B.C. Director-General, Si_ Ian Jacob, last night barred royalty critic, Mr. Malcolm Muggeridge, from appearing on television. Mr. Muggeridge was scheduled to appear in the Panorama programme last night to talk about the article he wrote for Saturday Evening Post, in which he described the Queen _umpish."

_sman who told _ of the ban said _ve should not _icity to a sub-

Night of t for Mugg

Special to the Auckland Star—From

MR MUGGERIDGE AND THE MONARCHY

Interview on American Television

FROM ALISTAIR COOKE : NEW YORK, Sunday

Like a proconsul summoned to Rome to explain the _ in East Anglia, Mr Malcolm Muggeridge flew into New Yo_ last night to account for his views on the British monarchy Mike Wallace, the public prosecutor of American televisi In one year Mr Wallace has bounded from obscurity _ portentous fame. He is a handsome, coltish young man seat_ in a black void, whose shady _ secrets he will expose befo_ the night is through.

"Night Beat" was the title of _ show that made him celebrated _ title that carried power_ ambiguous associations with a c_ on the prowl, dirty work at t_ crossroads, the midnight poundin_ of the stubborn suspect in th_ interest, of course, of all good me_ and true.

Strong men have quailed an_ wept when exposed to Mik_ _'s cross-examination. Fas_ _ and

MUGGERIDGE FLIES TO U.S. FOR TV SHOW

From JEFFREY BLYTH

NEW YORK, Thursday.
MR. Malcolm Muggeridge is flying to New York tomorrow to discuss his attack on the Queen on American television.

He will appear on the A.B.C Saturday night interview pr_ _ His inquisitor will _ _ _ e the most search American

A NICE THIS MUGGEI

By DONALD AD

SO Malcolm Muggeridge, th_ viewers love to hate, will _ tiny silver screen because of b_ Queen in an American magazine.

'Apologise' slogans at Muggeridge home

A N official of the League _ Empire Loyalists in _ _ said that_

"I shall never again write on monarchy"
— Mr. Muggeridge
NEW YORK, Monday.

Muggeridge

MALCOLM MUGGERIDGE and Sir Ian Jacob, director-General of the B.B.C., made it up yesterday.

They met to discuss Sir Ian's stopping Mr. Muggeridge's appearance in the B.B.C.s television programme _Panoram_ on Monday.

The B.B.C. said after th_ meeting: "There is _ Mr. Muggeridge. _ tinue to appear _ grammes."

So ends four sto_ Mr. Muggeridge _ he received teleph_ letters in protes_

"MUGGERIDGE AND HIS TRIBE" ATTACKED

568

Monarchy will outlast all their criticism, Australian M.P.s told

SOUTH AFRICAN PRESS ASSOCIATION-REUTER
CANBERRA Frida_

_Evening Post has been criticised.
Today, boarding a plane to return to London, he was asked if he would write furth_

Malcolm's Morbid Fascination
A TV Ogre Who Spe

Mu
568
on

From w
A WASH_ _ on Ma_ not carry a_ _arent netw_

umph
ridge
ridge,

'AIR COOKE

AN
Mr
DGE

millions of TV
barred from the
criticising the

No TV ban on Muggeridge
—SAYS B.B.C.

By JACK BELL

THE B.B.C. climbed down yesterday over the case of Malcolm Muggeridge.

An announcement from Broadcasting House last night said: "There is no ban on Mr. Muggeridge who will continue to appear in B.B.C. programmes."

This decision came after a day of discussion which began with a forty-minute talk between the Mr. Muggeridge and the B.B.C.'s Director-General, Sir Ian Jacob.

They met to discuss Sir Ian's ban on Mr. Muggeridge appearing in last Monday's TV programme "Panorama" to explain his views on The Queen and the Monarchy.

The ban followed publication in Britain of extracts from an article about the Queen which Mr. Muggeridge wrote for an American magazine.

Americans put TV blackout on critic of Queen

MALCOLM MUGGERIDGE said in New York yesterday that he feels "neither shame nor regret" over his "Saturday Evening Post" article on the Queen.

But when he arrived by plane from London for his appearance on an American Broadcasting Company's TV programme he was told:

"IT WILL NOT BE RELAYED TO WASHINGTON."

Reason? The Queen is there as the guest of President Eisenhower.

Muggeridge says: She's delightful

NEW YORK, Saturday. — Mr. Malcolm Muggeridge, in a TV interview here tonight gave "an emphatic yes" to the question: "Does England really need a Queen?" That was the title of the article he wrote for the Saturday Evening Post.

"The monarchial institution in England is immensely valuable," he said. "and the present incumbent is a very delightful exponent of that institution, and it would be a thousand pities if the institution allowed to collapse."

MR. MUGGERIDGE NOT ON WASHINGTON BROADCAST

FROM OUR OWN CORRESPONDENT

WASHINGTON, Oct. 18

television station that was interview with Mr.
row night has
manager con-
able

MONARCHY IS "PURE SHOW," SAYS BRITISH WRITER

UNDER the headline "Does England Really Need a Queen?— Elizabeth II is popular but powerless," the weekly magazine "Saturday Evening Post," with a circulation approaching 10 million, devotes pages of its next edition to an article by Mr. Malcolm Muggeridge, until recently editor of "Punch", and a British television personality.

Mr. Muggeridge's article

'Malicious,' says Muggeridge

NEW

BBC patch it up

By DOUGLAS MARLBOROUGH

ing the Queen in an can magazine.
was because of the article Sir Ian stopped his disng it on *Panorama*.

il yesterday the B.B.C. saying: "Mr. Muggeridge's future appearances under consideration."
en came the 60-minute ng "It was very friendly," idge said.
fs also met er to

Mal
here
that
the
ning
of
ind
his

ing to hear what happens about his B.B.C. contract": his 12-month contract ends in December.

Mr. Muggeridge said: "I have always been very happy with the B.B.C. Of course, I would have considered any lucrative offer if things hadn't turned out like this."

On October 30 he will be commentator in a film programme marking B.B.C. TV's 21st birthday.

eridge banned
ashington TV

BROADBENT: Washington, Friday.
television station has put a ban
Muggeridge. It said today it would
nterview with him, planned by it
tomorrow night

inds Britons

ITV scouts wait to sign up Muggeridge

By Philip Phillips

THE future of Malcolm Muggeridge so far as it affects his BBC career may be decided today when Mr. Muggeridge meets Sir Ian Jacob, Director-General of the BBC, in his office in London's Broadcasting House.

Sir Ian telephoned Mr.

TELE-PARADE

Muggeridge at his London flat last night and asked him to call today.

Mr. Muggeridge is due to appear in the Light Programme's "Any Questions" item from Worthing on November 1.
The B.B.C. could not say last

night whether he would be heard.

ITV companies are awaiting the outcome of Mr. Muggeridge's talk on the carpet of Sir Ian's office with great interest.

If Sir Ian declares Mr. Muggeridge's contract null and void he will at once be offered new contracts by ITV companies.

Last night the B.B.C. declared that about 200 letters and tele-

The 'Monarchy' imbroglio, being banned by the BBC, and having, of course, departed from *Punch*, left me, suddenly, with no gainful means of employment. For after *Punch* I was relying on the television work, particularly with *Panorama* (see page 72) with which I had increasingly been occupied, to earn the daily bread. Luckily, though, I was invited to Australia for a few months – to tour the country for the *Sydney Morning Herald* and to interview distinguished Australians on television. In the event it was one of these, Dr H.V. Evatt, Leader of the Opposition, who helped me to get a visa to China where I spent a month. From China I flew, without let or hindrance, to Moscow where things did not seem to have changed much since 1933.

Two pictures taken during my visit to Moscow at the time of Harold Macmillan's official visit in 1959.

70

Later in 1958 I went to cover the United Nations in New York. It felt like a loony bin in a world gone mad. In the US I met various people including Governor Orval Faubus at Little Rock, and Senator Hubert Humphrey. What with these travels, and a visit to the Berlin Wall, my year off seemed to have made it easier for newspapers and even the BBC to contemplate using me again; and in 1959 I was sent to report the visit of Harold Macmillan, the Prime Minister, to the Soviet Union. I even met Nikita Khruschev and discussed humour with him, he as a reader of *Krokodil*. We did not quite agree – he was one of nature's blimps – a blimpski, if you like.

It was now that television became the dominant *motif* in my life, and for the better part of the next ten years.

I always used to feel, even in Moscow, that Harold Macmillan had a tiny, tiny flavour of mothballs about him. Trog drew this cartoon of 'McMothballs' for *Muggeridge through the Microphone* (BBC, 1967).

This photo taken in 1960 shows some of the strain, perhaps, of the freelance journalist's, and controversialist's, life!

It had been during my time in Washington that I had my first experience of television from the performing side. During a discussion of the sovreignty of Israel between a Jew and an Arab, the two men became so heated that they shouted continuously at each other and neither could be heard. All I could do, as the English piggy-in-the-middle chairman, was to spread my hands and say straight to camera – 'You see what it is like!' However, it taught me the essential lessons of broadcasting, especially television – 'talk quietly, never shout, and look at the camera'. There are really no other lessons to learn.

On radio I began on programmes such as *The Critics* and *The Brains Trust* in Britain. My first talk, a portrait of Beatrice Webb, received such hostile criticism that George Barnes, Director of the Spoken Word at the BBC, apologized publicly on the BBC's behalf though not on mine.

Television was not a major influence in the UK until 1953, when the Coronation was seen by so many millions; thereafter the majority of homes possessed sets. It was at this point that I became involved with the first BBC *Panorama* programmes.

Panorama was the first major and successful serious television programme about politics and current affairs. It was advertised as 'A Window on the World', but when I first went to the studio what struck me most forcibly was that there were *no* windows. Obviously; but it underlined television's tendency to breed its own hothouse atmosphere. I did not get on very well, as it happened, with Richard Dimbleby, the programme's anchor-man and compère. On one occasion we were doing a feature on *1984*, George Orwell's novel, and as it ended and I had to hand over to Dimbleby, I said 'Over to Big Brother'. It was a silly joke, and I meant nothing by it. But he never forgave me.

I had different sorts of assignments on *Panorama*: one of the most potentially embarrassing was with the Irish playwright, Brendan Behan. This was a particularly difficult interview for me, as not only had Behan drunk a good deal on this occasion before he reached the BBC, he also tanked up generously on BBC hospitality. But in those days, when we went out live, you could not just cancel a feature – there was nothing available to substitute for it. The show had to go on! Which it did with me asking the questions, waiting for a grunt by way of reply, and then interpreting the grunt by giving the answer to my question myself. We just managed to win through, without Behan demanding to go and 'have a leak'.

Later Joan Littlewood told me she had completely failed to get any expressions of interest in Behan's play *The Quare Fellow* until he appeared drunk on television. Then they poured in.

Brendan Behan with Joan Littlewood, 1961.

In 1960 Granada Television commissioned from me a series of interviews under the title 'An Appointment with . . .' This lasted for some two years and my 'victims' included Arthur Miller, Jacques Soustelle (whom I had known in Paris in 1944), Lord Chandos, J.B. Priestley, Rev. G.L. Dwyer, Sir Harold Nicolson, Professor J.D. Bernal and Marian Anderson.

On another occasion I interviewed a famous literary quartet, W.H. Auden, Cyril Connolly, Christopher Isherwood and Stephen Spender. At yet another time I talked in the frankest of fashions with Sir Oswald Mosley – frank questions and frank answers – but the programme was never shown.

I used also to appear regularly on Granada's *Who goes next?* It appals me now, but I used to look uncommonly self-satisfied, and not a little arrogant.

Jacques Soustelle.

Arthur Miller.

J.B. Priestley.

74

Who goes next?, a regular Granada programme, with Richard Crossman (top), myself and Peter Thorneycroft.

I am caught in the midst of preparations for a programme and, slightly theatrically, 'savouring a point'.

RIGHT Perhaps I was asking for it when I said to the famous hostess Elsa Maxwell, 'Have you met any unimportant people?' Anyway, she replied, 'Not until tonight!'

Early in its turbulent life, *Private Eye* invited Claud Cockburn and myself to act as guest editors of the magazine, supplying our experience to their radical enthusiasm. The picture of those days shows Claud Cockburn between John Wells (left) and Richard Ingrams. Among the others are Peter Cook standing behind and Christopher Booker on his left.

It was around this time that Kim Philby, who had been my ultimate MI6 boss when I was in Mozambique during the war, was revealed as the 'third man' as he went to Russia to join Guy Burgess and Donald Maclean. The story dominated press and television and, in a way, has scarcely ceased to do so since.

That Philby could be a double agent, or a traitor, never even crossed my mind any more than it crossed the minds of his superiors or colleagues. Looking back, it is possible to sense, perhaps, in his frenetic drinking and womanizing, and even in his crippling stutter, some evidence for his split loyalties or dissatisfaction with his chosen path; yet Kim was always so much more interested in practice than theory that I have never been able to see him as a Marxist. What, indeed, remains a continuing puzzle is why these three men – Guy Burgess, Donald Maclean, and Philby – and also Anthony Blunt acted as they did. If one looks at the social conditions in Britain during the early twentieth century, one might expect lowly-paid and exploited workers to rebel. But they never did.

I remember how, on one delegation to Moscow, one working trade unionist was asked what he wanted to see, and chose a Russian mine; something he understood. The fact that ever afterwards he never had a good word to say for Russia or the Russian Revolution is evidence of what he must have found down that mine.

The upper-class traitors and their fellow-travellers were also looking for something they wanted to see. But, in their case, without objective proofs, they found only what they wanted to find and did not bother to test it. Why on earth? It seems to me that the paradox lies precisely in their position of comparative wealth and privilege. The man who has no social position or financial freedom lacks the time and opportunity, and the natural cover, to rebel. The richer and more privileged have these opportunities while their education may let them think of themselves as citizens of the world rather than

of one country. Their feet, and their loyalties, are no longer planted on the ground. However, it would have been a remarkable coup on the Russians' part if they had ever managed to infiltrate their man to the head of MI6; and they were not so far from doing that.

Many years later when I visited Moscow to make a television documentary, I asked if I, as an old friend, could visit Kim Philby. The reply I was given was, 'We are sorry. We do not know his address.' At the time I laughed. But now it seems a sad epitaph for those well-bred features.

When I once again became persona grata at the BBC I continued with interviews and branched out into special features. As time went by the interviews tended to become longer and more politically important. Among those people I interviewed were Cardinal Heenan, Pandit Nehru, David Ben-Gurion, Kurt Hahn, Leonard Woolf, and there were three whole programmes with Lord Reith, the 'founder' of the BBC. Among features I particularly felt were timely were 'Twilight of Empire', which took me back to India to record the end of the Raj; 'A hard bed to lie on', a study of a Cistercian monastery at Nunraw, near Edinburgh; and 'Paul – Envoy Extraordinary' made with my old friend Alec Vidler.

During the Second Vatican Council I was able to film Cardinal Heenan, Archbishop of Westminster, in the Vatican Gardens (below left). We had begun the programme at a lunch in Archbishop's House, when, since he was being attended by two nuns, I asked him 'Do they go with your job?' On another occasion I remarked to him that he had never invited me to become a Catholic. He responded, laughing, 'It would have been disastrous if you had!'

He came of Irish extraction and was previously Archbishop of Liverpool. Broadly conservative in outlook, he understood nevertheless that changes had to come; but he pointed out the role of the Church: 'We're the one thing in a changing world that is solid. We're the thing that people can reach for.' And he added: 'Some of us have got to stand quite firm and say, "Yes, I love this open view, but we mustn't for a moment forget truth, we musn't pretend that truth doesn't matter."'

My interview with Pandit Nehru (opposite) took place not very long before he died. He was a highly intelligent man of great charm who, because he was so Westernized (Harrow, Cambridge, etc.), did not perhaps understand India all that intimately although he certainly cared immensely about his country.

A constant theme of his talk was that Partition had been a disaster and should never have taken place in the way it had. He of course at that time (1947–8) had been hungry for power, as had Congress; and the Viceroy, Mountbatten, under orders from the Attlee government, was anxious to settle the problem of India as quickly as possible; so much so that when the Moslem leader, Jinnah, first heard about the policy, he disbelieved it. If only the British had said, we will hand over power when you have established proper governments and areas of influence, a tremendous number of lives, lost in the Partition riots, would have been saved.

When I went to see David Ben-Gurion (above), Israel's first (socialist) Prime Minister was living not in richness or in style, but simply, on a kibbutz.

We went for several walks together during the afternoons. As we did so, I occasionally noticed heads popping up around us from behind walls and banks and disappearing, and realized we were being very carefully guarded. He was pessimistic about the future, fearing that Israel would not enjoy the stability in which to develop evenly and naturally. He more than anyone else had introduced the use of Hebrew as the national language, and the idea, whatever its difficulties, certainly helped in imposing a sense of unity on people, all Jews, but of very disparate origins.

In passing, I happened to mention that Kim Philby had defected. His comment was sharp: since Kim's father, H. St John Philby, an adviser to Ibn Saud, had become a Moslem, why should Kim not become a Russian?

An unexpected and impressive man whom I interviewed and greatly liked was Kurt Hahn, with his well-balanced ideas on the *mens sana in corpore sano* view of education. He it was, as founder and headmaster of Gordonstoun, who took Prince Charles into the school and also arranged for him to go to Tree Top in Australia. He was co-founder of the Outward Bound Sea School in Wales. He looked like a typical, heavy German, and proved to be partly Jewish, thoughtful, intelligent, and humane.

I thought very highly of Leonard Woolf (below), both as a man and as a writer. He was pleasant and clever, yet it seemed to me that he was never given his due, never properly valued by the other members of the Bloomsbury Group. Indeed he was actually under-valued, perhaps because he was in part Jewish, perhaps because he so worshipped Virginia – in both a literary and a social sense. He tended her devotedly, protecting her as best he could – even, on one occasion, as he told me, taking a whole hour to coax her to eat a spoonful of food. Shortly after he and I had done our programme together in 1969 (the year he died) he gave a garden party at Rodmell, and four times as many people turned up, he told me, as had come to previous such occasions.

One of the most remarkable interviews I did was with Lord Reith (opposite). He was a most impressive and curiously touching human individual. Physically he was immensely tall – Churchill once referred to 'that wuthering height'; Reith himself said to me that being very tall was 'as much of a deformity as being a dwarf'.

Having been brought up as the son of a Presbyterian minister, he had a strong religious nature, so much so that he almost came to regard himself as someone 'destined to carry out the wishes of Our Lord'. It was this fundamental sense of mission that informed his creation of the BBC; yet with it he combined a constant feeling of being inadequate.

He was appointed to this job (he simply replied to an advertisement) because of his training as an engineer. While this was, of course, valuable in the setting up of a completely new organization for which there was no precedent, it was his intellectual and spiritual qualities – rather than his technical ones – which were to be the hallmark and nature of broadcasting, and of his dream to use radio to 'elevate'. He also used to say about this, commenting on the Abdication of Edward VIII, that 'broadcasting was making history'. This was not strictly true, perhaps, although it was certainly changing the way in which history was recorded.

Two things essentially come out of his creation of the BBC. First, he was confident that, when serious war came, he would be summoned to a high ministerial post by Churchill. This did not happen, and Reith was greatly hurt. Second, when television broke out of the BBC's Reithian mould, particularly with satirical programmes

things, he was a much disappointed man. Perhaps that is why to me he is a touching figure, because he was much too honest to hide it. And he kept saying that he had never been tested or 'properly stretched' by life.

I have two final glimpses of Reith.

The first is at Holyrood Palace in Edinburgh. He was representing the Queen in certain vice-regal ceremonies, and said to me, pointing to the surrounding flummery, 'All this is nonsense, of course'. The remark was genuinely felt. He may have wished in his life that he had not missed out on so much of the fun, but this was not it.

The second picture I find even more moving. At the end of our series of interviews, I persuaded him to read out aloud the last of his father's sermons – but he broke down with the emotion of doing so. This was never broadcast. Yet it would have made the perfect and significant end to his memorable appearance, precisely because he was so human.

like *That Was The Week That Was*, he was shocked. This was no role, as he saw it, for national broadcasting. Such programmes did not *elevate*. In this, as in other

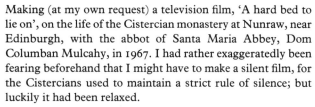

Making (at my own request) a television film, 'A hard bed to lie on', on the life of the Cistercian monastery at Nunraw, near Edinburgh, with the abbot of Santa Maria Abbey, Dom Columban Mulcahy, in 1967. I had rather exaggeratedly been fearing beforehand that I might have to make a silent film, for the Cistercians used to maintain a strict rule of silence; but luckily it had been relaxed.

LEFT TO RIGHT Eleanor Bron, Norman Shelley, James Roose-Evans, and David Hicks who designed the set.

Television is an all-sorts, bits and pieces type of job. In addition to interviews and features I might find myself doing a show with Mike Yarwood (opposite above) and offering hostages to the fortune of his brilliant impersonations (1966); or (opposite) leading a discussion programme on South Africa (1970) with Lord Alport, Professor Christiaan Barnard, Rt Rev. David Sheppard, and Peter Hain; or presenting 'An Evening with Malcolm Muggeridge', an anthology of favourite writings read for me by Eleanor Bron and Norman Shelley (the voice of Churchill and Pooh!)

I used to say that it all made me feel like a man playing a piano in a brothel – every now and again he solaces himself by playing 'Abide with Me' in the hope of edifying both the clients and the inmates. This inspired one of Trog's marvellous drawings (right) for *Muggeridge Ancient and Modern* (BBC, 1981).

During the 1960s I also became involved with films. It began with *I'm All Right, Jack*, the Boulting Brothers' film which starred Peter Sellers and in which I played a TV interviewer. That was one thing; but playing the admittedly small part of an archdeacon in *Heavens Above* was something quite else even though I wrote the original story and screenplay myself. Roy and John Boulting, who had had so much success satirizing aspects of British life, had asked me, 'How can we be funny about the Christian religion?'

Peter Sellers I found to be an extraordinary contrast. As a character actor, for example as the shop steward in *I'm All Right, Jack*, he was superbly funny and sharp in his portrayal. A wonderful 'turn'. When I later came to interview him as himself, however, he proved to be banal and a bore. He was only funny when he was someone else. I cannot help feeling that it was this gap between his performances and his own character which so distressed him that he would drown his feelings in drink, drugs and womanizing. He was too intelligent not to sense it. In a way, too, his tragedy was that he was less an actor than an impersonator – but what marvellous impersonations! Compared to Charles Chaplin he created mannerism rather than character.

I have never forgotten the episode when Chaplin is taking his dog for a walk, only to be confronted by the notice NO DOGS ALLOWED. Immediately all the Chaplin anarchy and ingenuity are brought into play as he places the dog out of sight down his trousers. But thereby hangs a tail. Charlie has forgotten the hole in the seat of his trousers.

This is typical of Chaplin's comic style which enlarges so richly on the character of the tramp and his dress that Chaplin remembered from his youth in a very poor part of London. But Chaplin never made the mistake – which sometimes Peter Sellers did – of laughing at his own humour. He knew how much funnier it was played straight.

Alice in Wonderland is a book which I have never liked but it has always fascinated me. So I was delighted to be invited to play the Gryphon in Jonathan Miller's film. And here I am, and here too is Sir John Gielgud as the Mock Turtle, and Anne-Marie Mallik as Alice, dancing the Lobster Quadrille.

I was much amused by Geoffrey Moorhouse's comment in the *Guardian*: 'Mr Muggeridge's whole life has been leading up to the evening when he would dance a dab-toed quadrille before a carefully prepared audience, against a sky of gathering gloom.' What he means, I suppose, is that I'm an old ham.

In 1966 I was invited to stand for election as the Rector of Edinburgh University. The other three candidates were John Mackintosh MP; Lord Dunsany, Chairman of the Scottish Land Court; and Quintin Hogg, now Lord Hailsham; but I got a very handsome vote. I think the students were enthusiastic that they had elected an irreverent agnostic, but in my Rectorial address I tried to turn their thoughts towards the truths of the Christian religion.

The Rector's job is not a sinecure or an honorific appointment. He has some ceremonial functions; but primarily he is there to represent the students on and to the governing body of the university. In my case it all started to go wrong when a demand came from the students that free birth control pills should be made available to all female students, following on the suspension of the editor of the student magazine for advocating the use of dangerous levels of the drug LSD. Since I had to represent the students' views, but could not support them, the only course I could take was to resign. My three-year term had lasted, sadly, but one year.

The first person to publish a condemnation of my attitude was a Roman Catholic chaplain. I felt at the time that he was due to become a bishop – and he did. But it gave me my first taste of controversy inside the Catholic Church.

This was a time when I constantly seemed to be addressing public issues publicly. Above, I am speaking to the Conference of the Institute of Directors in the Albert Hall in 1968. On the right, I am preaching in 1970 in one of the twin pulpits of the church of St Mary-le-Bow. The debate between Enoch Powell and myself was on the text of what should be rendered to Caesar and what to God. Part of the discussion focused on the system of Apartheid:

MUGGERIDGE   Can it be right that any person should be regarded as inferior for any purpose?

POWELL   I think you have confused 'separate' and 'inferior'. The arguments for separation would be just as valid if those who were to be separated were regarded as superior.

MUGGERIDGE   But they are not.

87

Images of myself. I watch Karin Jonzin as she puts finishing touches to the bust which was presented to me in 1963 by Leslie Illingworth, the cartoonist.

Illingworth and myself, old friends and colleagues.

LEFT I meet a half-familiar figure in Madame Tussaud's in 1968. I wonder, would I have recognized myself?

A portrait in oils by Nina Guppy. I particularly like the black cap, which was given to me by my friend Father Bidone. He spent most of a lifetime protecting mongoloid children in their lives, and against those who felt that those lives were not worth living. One of his projects left unfinished at his death in 1986 was a school, to be set up in Jordan, for Christian and Mohammedan boys to be educated together. God rest his soul.

Trog's splendid cartoon of St Mugg. Could I ever have been a saint?

A snapshot, taken in 1968, of my brothers – from right to left, Eric, Jack, Douglas and myself; and (opposite) a delightful portrait of Kitty by Michael Ward.

In the course of filming 'A Life of Christ', in 1967, during which I was able to see the reality of Jesus' wilderness, the desert (above), I visited the Church of the Nativity in Bethlehem. And it was here that I received the first intimation of conversion – a mystical feeling, a sense of being someone else and of some other way of life not connected with the ego's pursuits. I may have been on the stage of the Holy Land, but the play was Jesus himself.

I remember the precise moment of illumination. I was sitting in the crypt waiting for the time when the public was excluded and we could begin to film. Earlier in the day we had been filming in nearby fields where, reputedly, shepherds were tending their flocks when they heard the tidings of great joy. Sure enough, in the fields there was a shepherd with his flock – sheep and goats duly separated, just as required. When he caught sight of us and our equipment he picked up one of his sheep in his arms, precisely as in the coloured pictures I remembered so well from Scripture lessons in my childhood. Then, when he had established his posture, and our cameraman was focusing for a shot, he put down the sheep and came forward to haggle over his fee.

It was after settling this unseemly transaction, and getting our footage of the shepherd and his flock, that we went into the Church of the Nativity, having the greatest difficulty in making our way because of the press of beggars and children offering picture postcards, rosaries and other souvenirs for sale.

I had found a seat in the crypt on a stone ledge in the shadow cast by the lighted candles which provided the only illumination. How ridiculous these so-called 'shrines' were, I was thinking to myself. How squalid the commercialism which exploited them! Who but a credulous fool could possibly suppose that the place marked in the crypt with a silver cross was veritably the spot where Jesus had been born? The Holy Land, it seemed to me, had been turned into a sort of Jesusland, on the lines of Disneyland.

As these thoughts passed through my mind I began to notice the demeanour of the visitors coming into the crypt. Some crossed themselves; a few knelt down; most were obviously standard twentieth-century pursuers of happiness for whom the Church of the Nativity was just one item in a sight-seeing tour – as it might be the Taj Mahal, or Madame Tussaud's, or Lenin's mausoleum.

Nonetheless, each face as it came into view was in some degree transfigured by the experience of being in what purported to be the actual place of Jesus' birth. This was where it happened, they all seemed to be saying. Here He came into the world! Here we shall find Him! The boredom, the idle curiosity, the vagrant thinking all disappeared. Once more in that place glory shone around, and angel voices proclaimed: *Unto you is born this day . . . a Saviour, which is Christ the Lord!*, thereby transforming it from a tourist attraction into an authentic shrine.

Where two or three are gathered together in my name, Jesus promised, *there I am in the midst of them.* The promise has been kept even in the unlikeliest of places – His own ostensible birthplace.

It is written in the Old Testament that no man may see God and live; at the same time, as Kierkegaard points out, God cannot make man His equal without transforming him into something more than man. The only solution was for God to become man, which He did through the Incarnation in the person of Jesus. Thereby He set a window in the tiny dark dungeon of the ego in

The Church of the Nativity in Bethlehem.

which we all languish, letting in a light, providing a vista, and offering a way of release from the servitude of the flesh and the fury of the will into what St Paul called 'the glorious liberty of the children of God'.

This is what the Incarnation, realized in the birth of Jesus, and in the drama of His ministry, death and resurrection, was to signify. With it Eternity steps into Time, and Time loses itself in Eternity. Hence Jesus; in the eyes of God, a man, and, in the eyes of men, a God. It is sublimely simple; a transcendental soap opera going on century after century in which there have been endless variations in the script, in the music, in the dialogue, but in which one thing remains constant – the central figure, Jesus.

93

In 1967 I published *Jesus Rediscovered*. I was in fact somewhat apprehensive because the book was not one sustained, coherent utterance as a book ideally should be, but a collection of essays written for journals as different as the *New Statesman* and *The Ladies' Home Journal*, *The Christian Century* and the *Daily Telegraph* magazine. It was my publishers, Collins, who persuaded me to make the collection and their judgement was certainly vindicated for it became a bestseller. 'All I can claim,' I wrote in the Foreword, 'is that my thoughts and reflections on the Christian religion represent the sincere and sustained effort of one ageing, twentieth-century mind to give expression to a deep dissatisfaction with prevailing contemporary values and assumptions, and an abiding sense, ever more overwhelming in its intensity, that there is an alternative – an alternative that was first propounded two thousand years ago near the Sea of Galilee. . . .'

I added a sort of disclaimer then which is still valid: 'The theological implications of this position, I should explain, are quite beyond me. Theology is one of those subjects, like algebra and thermodynamics, in which I have never been able to interest myself. I am a theological ignoramus.'

When, a few years later, I was making another film in and around the Middle East on 'Paul – Envoy Extraordinary' I was lucky to have the companionship and participation of Alec Vidler. With his knowledge of the New Testament he was able to keep us straight on the historical and theological aspects, such as when Paul, in Athens, did not make a success of his preaching. I likened the scholars and intellectuals of Athens who refused to listen to his message to 'dons too learned to understand'. Alec riposted, 'They were not like dons but like journalists!'

OPPOSITE Heaven alone knows why I am standing here at the memorial to Karl Marx in Highgate Cemetery and laughing. After all, Marx and Freud are the two great destroyers of Christian civilization, the first replacing the gospel of love by the gospel of hate, the other undermining the essential concept of human responsibility. And Marx could also be called 'The God that Failed'. Nothing funny about that.

Sometime in 1969 I received a call from the BBC Religious Department (Radio). 'There is an Indian female, a nun of sorts, doing good works in Calcutta. You know Calcutta. Would you like to come and see her and find out what this is all about?'

Mother Teresa is Albanian, in fact. She belongs to an Order called the Missionaries of Charity, and originally she came to India by being given passage as a stewardess. She had never been interviewed before. However, she told me about her work which she described as being centred on 'a ministry to the poorest of the poor' – lepers, the starving, the homeless, outcasts, including the children who lived in the big railway stations.

I was impressed. The producer was impressed. Our listeners were impressed – so much so that they produced an unparalleled response. Clearly something very important was occurring.

Mother Teresa was trying to offer 'something beautiful for God', but her approach was so human. Beggars are not authorized in Calcutta, but she would say to them, 'How much did you get today?' or 'Did you have a good day?'

She herself accepts money only for 'the poorest of the poor'. And she does not accept the spending of money by her nuns even to print a prayer book. No accounts are kept. There is no organization in any formal sense. 'Surely, Mother Teresa,' a businessman once said, 'you must have a budget?' 'All right,' she replied, 'you be my budget.' Nor will she accept government aid. 'It means government interference.'

She has often been offered help by all sorts of friends, but her reaction has been 'I don't want friends, I want workers'. Thus was born the concept of the world-wide 'Co-workers of Mother Teresa'. Also she has a sixth sense of where her nuns and co-workers will next be needed. They are not sent out to run existing stations. They are sent out to create new ones and find what money they can however they can. In Mother Teresa's Home for the Dying Destitute, upper-caste people are expected to perform such tasks as cutting toe-nails and laying out. Mother Teresa always acts instinctively as though there is no system, or no facilities such as a mortuary. And she has never refused a child.

She was always very keen that I should become a Catholic, although she tends to grumble about the Catholic hierarchy. But then she remembers – 'Jesus himself handpicked twelve apostles: one betrayed him and the others ran away. So if Jesus can't do better . . .' I have not seen her recently and she has had a heart attack, but her work continues and has been enormously influential. She gets co-workers into most countries, including the USA and Latin America. The only place where her writ seems not to run is Northern Ireland.

I wrote *Something Beautiful for God* which has been translated into nearly every language and all its earnings have been passed on to Mother Teresa. She is still anxious lest her movement become too formalized and will not appoint a successor. She simply says, in her straight-forward way, 'If God wants our work to continue, it will continue. If he doesn't, it won't.'

That practical Christianity is one thing I particularly associate with her. The other is an incident when we, BBC Television, were filming *Something Beautiful for God* in the former Hindu temple which was being used as the Home for the Dying Destitute in Calcutta. Our cameraman, a hard-bitten professional named Ken Macmillan, said, 'It is too dark in here.' Nonetheless he decided to have a go. He expected his film to go black because of the inadequacy of the light. Actually, when the film was processed, it appeared to shed a soft light which, in workaday terms, could not be realized. Ken Macmillan has left an account of what happened in the hope that it might ultimately assist in the canonization of Mother Teresa. In the event, he was quite unable to account for how the film came out in perfect brightness.

This touching, almost heart-rending photograph of Svetlana – taken when she was staying at our house to record a memorable interview for television – seems to reveal all the tension and tragedy of being the daughter of Stalin, and so a displaced and almost unplaceable person in the modern world.

98

Unfortunately, since that time, our relations with Svetlana have been strained. She wanted to come and live in England around 1981 and asked my advice. I had to say then that it did not seem to me a propitious time for her to do so, what with the growing recession and unemployment. She thought, I believe, that I was trying to put her off, and wrote a bitter and hurtful letter to Kitty and me. She finally did come to England, but, in 1985, she obtained permission to return to Russia along with her daughter Olga who had been brought up in the USA and who would, inevitably, find Russia, and schooling there, difficult to handle. Svetlana was sent to Tiflis in Georgia.

Georgia, of course, was Stalin's home state; and Svetlana herself used to give us a marvellous reminiscence of him. At the time of her mother's death, Svetlana went to see her grandmother, Stalin's mother. 'What a pity Joseph did not stay on in his seminary,' the grandmother said to Svetlana. 'He would have made a wonderful priest.' It was almost as though his career had not prospered. Stalin himself used to dine out on the story.

Svetlana's mother in fact committed suicide because of Joseph's contemptuous treatment of her; but at least he walked behind her coffin at the funeral. Svetlana remembers him as a warm personality, a kindly father, when she was little; but inevitably she did not see much of him. On the other hand she sat all night by his deathbed in 1953 and recalls his last act – he raised his clenched fist up into the air, and died.

Svetlana was baptized when she was young, entirely of her own volition. This was a plucky thing to do with her father at the height of his power. She married, first, a Jew, also a brave act; then an ambitious doctor by whom she had two children; then she fell in love with a Sikh, who was a sick man but one of considerable spiritual force. When he died she carried his ashes to be scattered in the River Ganges, and stayed in India for a while, and then came to Europe to obtain a visa for the United States. It was at this time that, preoccupied with Christianity, she wrote a fan letter to me about *Jesus Rediscovered* to which I responded.

In the US she married a French architect and lived with him in a community created by Frank Lloyd Wright. Her daughter Olga was born when Svetlana was forty and, by then, separated from her husband. She wrote

two books about Russia, moved out of the community, and sent Olga to a Quaker school. She approached two Russian Orthodox churches in the US: one was virulently anti-Soviet; one refused to accept Stalin's daughter. Although she was helped by the Christian Scientists she was rootless.

She seems to me an utterly tragic person, living a life beyond bearing. She is often arrogant; but unstable too. Yet I will never forget the day when we played her a recording of the singing of the Russian Orthodox *Credo*. Her eyes filled with tears and she wept unconsolably.

Before Svetlana returned to Russia, Kitty and I received this letter from Olga:

Dear Mr and Mrs Muggeridge:
 Thank you dearly for your enchanting letter.
 In your letter you told me this: 'there's no reason why individuals shouldn't be happy and loving together'. But I'm afraid my mother and I aren't as happy and loving together as we are supposed to be. Please thank Mrs Muggeridge for her lovely gifts; especially the lead rope.

Sincerely,
(sgd) Olga Peters

Since we received that letter, Olga has returned to her school in England, and her mother has gone back to live in the United States.

"O.K., luv, Princess Alexandra has gone, but hang on a minute - here come Lord Longford and Malcolm Muggeridge."

RIGHT A delightful cartoon from Heath.
OPPOSITE A terrible warning from Giles.

"I DON'T CARE WHO HE SAYS HE IS, TELL MR MUGGERIDGE HE'LL HAVE TO WAIT HIS TURN LIKE EVERYBODY ELSE!"

BELOW If you believe in something, you should do something about it.

James Cameron and his wife Moni, with Kitty and myself, at our home in Robertsbridge when we were doing a programme together. James was a lovable man, a splendid journalist, yet rather a tragic figure, I felt. I sensed a conflict between his love of family and the gregariousness of the foreign correspondent whose nature was to be a loner. Somehow this was expressed by his dress at my 80th birthday party. He arrived in immaculate evening dress. By the end of the evening the tie was off, the shirt askew (see page 110), and he was more like his real self.

BELOW Kitty, Alec Vidler and myself on one of our favourite walks around Robertsbridge, which we name Australia. Somehow the landscape of this particular area seems to echo Australia rather than the normal gentleness and fertility of Sussex.

I have been friendly with Richard Ingrams since the early days of *Private Eye* (see page 77), but during his editorship it seemed he became bored with the magazine, especially when he said things like 'the biggest burden is sitting for hours and hours in the law courts'. On the other hand he appears happiest when he is playing the organ in his local church where perhaps the influence of his Catholic mother and his C of E father combine in his Christian nature. I find him an interesting mixture of toughness and (unnecessary) lack of confidence in his abilities.

When I was told he that he was going to write my biography I was very pleased. He has already written a sympathetic and perceptive study in *God's Apology* of the relationship between Hugh Kingsmill, Hesketh Pearson and myself. The most a subject can ask for in a biographer is a measure of affection that will produce insight and understanding whatever the final judgement.

In 1978 I gave an address to a Symposium in San Francisco to celebrate the tenth anniversary of the encyclical *Humanae Vitae*, known as the 'birth control' encyclical, of Pope Paul VI. The essence of that address is contained in this story of mine about Mother Teresa:

'A little baby had been brought in (to the children's clinic), so small that it seemed almost inconceivable that it could live. And I say rather fatuously to Mother Teresa, "When there are so many babies in Calcutta and in Bengal and in India, and so little to give to them, is it *really* worthwhile going to all this trouble to save this little midget?" And she picks up the baby and she holds it, and she says to me, "Look! There is life in her".'

That is also precisely what *Humanae Vitae* is about.

to be at the mercy of an atheistic, tyrannical regime. His great influence in Poland has, of course, been made the more effective there by his becoming Pope, for his experience makes him – when faced by hostile movements or undermining tactics such as 'liberation theology' in Latin America – the best champion to strengthen the authority of Pope and Church. And that strengthening is sorely needed in an irreligious, materialistic world, even at the cost of a certain conservatism.

Bishop Fulton Sheen was a revered figure in the United States. I remember him particularly for one remark he made to me which was almost a prophecy. 'Christendom is over,' he said, 'but not Christ.' He was very ill when we met, and he died shortly afterwards; but his observation remains with me.

I was privileged to meet Pope John Paul II when filming with William Buckley in the Sistine Chapel. The Pope is a brave man and a tough man, although I also felt that, not surprisingly, he did not really understand England and, indeed, understood English only phonetically. On the other hand, I think he is an admirable choice as Pope precisely because he has been a cardinal in a communist country and therefore knows at first hand what it means

I wish I could remember what exactly I was arguing in this picture taken at Bishop Otter College, Chichester in 1981, especially as I seem to be quietly persuasive!

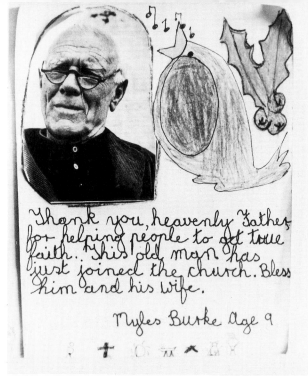

Thank you, heavenly Father for helping people to get true faith. This old man has just joined the church. Bless him and his wife.

Myles Burke Age 9

I had brooded over becoming a Roman Catholic for many years, and yet I, and Kitty too, had mysteriously held back. I have a vivid memory of walking around the Serpentine with Mother Teresa and discussing it. She was eager to see me a fellow Catholic; and I was as eager to please her, for she had given me a whole new vision of what being a Catholic means.

In our spiritual lives, some sort of subterranean process takes place whereby, after years of doubt and uncertainty, clarification and assurance suddenly emerge and, like the blind man whose sight Jesus restored, we say, 'One thing I know, that whereas I was blind, now I see'. This is what happened to me.

But then one needs to find out how and why – after the clarification, however, not as part of it.

First there is the Church, and its rituals, which has survived through 2000 years. Second, there are the saintly, from Paul to Mother Teresa and not forgetting my own favourite, Augustine of Hippo. His *Confessions* shows

Kitty and myself being greeted by Lord Longford, who sponsored our reception
into the Roman Catholic Church, after the service.

how worldliness and carnality can be transmuted into a
life of service to God, just as a present-day climate of
permissiveness can evoke a response like *Humanae Vitae*.
Such was the Catholic reaction to a moral crisis.

But there is something else to becoming a Catholic – a
sense of homecoming, of picking up the threads of a lost
life, of finding a place at table that has long been vacant.
All of this brings one closer to other Christians – and
nearer into the world-wide Christian fellowship. Thanks
be to God.

In recent years I have been a good deal in contact with William F. Buckley Jr. He is a leading US journalist, with a regular three-day-a-week column syndicated throughout the country; a prominent Catholic; the owner of his own radio station and with a talk-show called *Firing Line* which has been active for twenty years. It was in 1981 that we shared a debate on 'Faith and Religious Institutions' which covered two one-hour programmes. It started with our discussing 'doubt' – doubt, that is, as the dialectical partner of faith.

Bill Buckley has been described as a sort of Muggeridge of America, and I as the Buckley of England. I don't know, but Buckley is certainly a most attractive, honest and sincere practitioner. And if it was true that he was offered the US ambassadorship to London, we would have been fortunate. But he decided to retain his stake in discussing and challenging the progress of public events.

If he had wished it, Alexander Solzhenitsyn could have become the grand old man of letters in Russia and lived a time-honoured life there, especially after the publication of *One Day in the Life of Ivan Denisovitch*. Just as Gorki did. But Gorki, who had a villa in Italy, once said, 'There is no forced labour in Russia'. That is the sort of untruth Solzhenitsyn could never utter. On the contrary, he has fought the battle of the Zeks and he will continue to do so. He has never been happy in the USA. Would he be happy if he returned to Russia? Who can tell? But he remarked to me one day: 'I have no reason for saying this, but I am confident that before I die I shall return to Russia.' That would certainly fit in with his artistic ambitions. The Russian revolutionaries, he points out, destroyed Russian history. Solzhenitsyn's intention in his books is to give it back.

Visible from left to right: Christopher Booker, Philip Ziegler, Philip Howard, Hugh Cudlipp, Frank Johnson, Bill Deedes, Andrew Boyle, Father Bidone, Auberon Waugh, Terence Kilmartin, Alan Watkins, Richard Ingrams, Jonathan Stedall, John Wells, Rev. Michael Chantry, James Cameron and, in the seats of age and honour, myself and Alec Vidler.

On 25 March 1983 a special dinner was organized by Richard Ingrams at the Garrick Club in my honour. It was a joyous occasion for me. Happy and lucky is the man who can sit down, dine, talk and laugh with so many old friends, colleagues and sparring partners on any occasion, let alone his eightieth birthday.

I was presented by Trog with a marvellous cartoon which now hangs in my study.

Presented to
MALCOLM MUGGERIDGE
on his 80th birthday
The Garrick Club 25th March 1983

To Malcolm Muggeridge
With Best Wishes
& Warm Regards
Ronald Reagan

```
22 MAR 1984/1729

ZCZC DLM2376 NKY746 IOA112 1-008693J082

GBXX CO UDNX 044

TDWX GOVT WHITE HOUSE DC 44/43/22 1211


MR. MALCOLM MUGGERIDGE

PARK COTTAGE

ROBERTSBRIDGE

SUSSEXENGLAND


NANCY AND I SEND OUR WARM REGARDS ON YOUR BIRTHDAY.

WE WISH YOU THE VERY BEST ON YOUR SPECIAL DAY AND ALWAYS.

HAPPY BIRTHDAY, OUR REGARDS TO KITTY AND GOD BLESS YOU BOTH.

    RONALD REAGAN
```

This telegram of congratulation from President and Mrs Reagan was a thoughtful, kind gesture. So was the signed photograph taken after their conversation in Washington with Mother Teresa. Mr Reagan is sometimes described as insensitive, a bull at a gate. On this occasion, however, when a reporter asked him what they talked about, he replied, 'We didn't talk. We listened.'

PARK COTTAGE

We came to Park Cottage (on the left) in 1958, and
added the second cottage, which we call The Ark, in
1980. This became possible when I received an unexpected windfall and made one of the more sensible decisions
of my life in thus 'extending' Park Cottage with a complete, self-contained dwelling which has turned out to
possess a delightfully calm, friendly atmosphere. We
named The Ark after Jean Vannier's home for the dis-
abled called 'L'Arche'. Maybe his beneficent spirit pre-
sides over it along with the quiet spirit of the Cistercians
who once owned this land.

116

Park Cottage lies in farmland about one mile from Robertsbridge, and five miles from Battle, in East Sussex. It is a part of the country we know well and love, for we have lived hereabouts, on and off, since 1937, firstly at Whatlington which is eight miles away.

The following pages give an idea of how we live, of our routine and habits, through the pictures of Chris Barham who also lives in Robertsbridge, and who here is sorting through a selection of photographs with me.

For me, black and white photographs, especially when they are as good as these, capture the spirit of places and people more persuasively and sympathetically than does colour. I always remember asking a cameraman in one of my TV crews, what the green thing was under his arm. 'Oh,' he replied, 'that's the plastic grass, in case the real grass isn't green enough!'

Looking back towards Park Cottage, the view of the other (front) side, with our bedroom on the right, taken from the other side of the lane. The Ark is on the left.

We seldom seem to use this side except when going out for walks, for cars can more easily approach and park on the west side, despite the farm road!

Reveille, 5.00 a.m. For years now I have woken up at crack of dawn, if not earlier. Even in winter I find this interlude between waking up and starting the day a wonderfully quiet time for making fresh notes on the work I did the previous day. But I need a cup of tea.

What a pleasure it is to look out over our always welcoming view from the bedroom window, and to watch the phases of the year as they change. A wonderful escape from the world of mechanisms.

One of the first jobs of the day, in summer, is to go and see what the hens have done for us – eggs being crucial in the vegetarian diet. In winter, of course, the hens need more time – so then we leave the job till evening.

Mike Pearce serves coffee at my local pub, the Seven Stars. With me are Mike Lyons and David Boorman (right).

We love getting letters, but we receive more than we can ever hope to answer.

Shopping in Robertsbridge. Robertsbridge is quite a small village, but it is cut in two by the A21 London-to-Hastings road on which the traffic is fast, heavy and menacing. Hence Kitty's and my frantic glances as we seek to cross back to 'our' side of the High Street.

I once approached the police about the danger. 'We can't do anything,' they told me, 'unless there is a fatal accident.' I thought of putting an advertisement in *The Times*, or writing to 'Exit', saying: 'If anyone is contemplating ending their lives, will they please come to the corner of Robertsbridge High Street and Fair Lane . . .'

We are lucky in our friendly shopkeepers – Ken Aubrey and Winston Rogers, the butchers; Stan Steadman, the chemist; and Robin King and the ladies in the Robertsbridge Store. Between them they supply most of what we need and even some things, like the chicken, or the beer in the trolley, which we don't, but which our guests enjoy. Supermarket-style shops have completely justified themselves, but I remember the protests when their arrival caused several smaller shops to close.

Home for lunch, a pleasure all the more welcome for us since it hardly ever varies. Kitty and I have been vegetarians since the time we came here in 1958. Kitty makes her own bread, usually brown, and her own yoghurt, and we eat a lot of salad, cheese and fruit. And a Fox's glacier mint with the coffee afterwards.

125

After lunch I like to retire to my study and talk, then resume work. Ever since I left the *Daily Telegraph* and *Punch*, and of course before then too, I have worked as a free-lance – in journalism, as an author, and in television. The free-lance life certainly has its compensations, but one thing I never feel able to do is relax and turn down jobs that are offered. You might think that, after the age of seventy or more, this instinct would diminish; but I assure you, old habits die hard. And when you are in my position – having changed jobs so often that I do not qualify for a pension – the automatic reaction is to accept.

126

My friends tell me I talk with my hands.

My study walls are festooned with photographs and cartoons – memories of all sorts of different friends and occasions from over the years. On the right, is the Sutherland sketch for his portrait of Somerset Maugham.

Opposite, Chris Barham has caught me out posing like a preacher under Trog's vision of St Mugg, which he rather rudely spells with one 'g'! It is brilliantly drawn, caricaturing my belated adoption of a Christian position.

I do a lot of walking, sometimes on favourite paths in the lanes and fields around the house, sometimes to the village. Here I might sit for a while at the top of the High Street (despite the traffic) under the 'arms' of Roberts-bridge, or meet and talk with our local vicar, John Lambourne, and interrupt his jogging.

Of course, there are other things to be done at home, such as mowing the lawn. The sheer peacefulness of living in the country is sometimes underlined by such activity and Kitty, watching here, seems to be sensing this.

We use The Ark as an extra study, for working on special projects, for meetings, parties, and for our guests, including our family; for though quite small, it is spacious and self-contained. Kitty and I also frequently enjoy our tea there.

Still, they tell me, the bright blue eyes
of the Mellin's baby.

At weekends, we often have visits from our family. This
occasion in 1983 was a sort of late celebration for my
eightieth birthday, with different members of the family
coming from as far afield as Holland and Canada.

On such occasions, Grandpa gets inveigled by his Canadian grandchildren, Matthew and Peter, to practise baseball throwing and catching. Happily they don't seem to mind my congenital incompetence at ball-games!

137

Out for a stroll with Kitty.

Later, it will be back to my study and my typewriter – perhaps to try and catch up on some of our letters. Even with Kitty's help I am always behind with them.

We like to play a game of chess, just as we used to do in Cairo (page 26).

We also read a lot together.

Every evening, before we go to bed, Kitty and I have a
quiet time together for prayer and meditation.

OPPOSITE I still enjoy going for walks, whatever the weather.

'I have lived long enough: my way of life
Is fall'n into the sear, the yellow leaf.' *Macbeth* v,3

Acknowledgements for the photographs

Aberdeen Journals Ltd 35
Abbot Hall Art Gallery, Kendal 27
Associated Press 65 right, below
BBC 71 left; 73; 78 left and right; 79; 80 above and below; 82 right, above; 90 left; 92; 96; 97; 98; 99; 109
BBC Hulton Library 34 right; 38; 39 right; 43; 49 right, above; 54; 60; 61; 64–5 centre (photo Bert Hardy)
Camera Press 56; 75 left, below and centre (photo Tom Blau); 77
Howard Coster 33
Daily Mail 65 left, above; 82 left, above and below; 86; 87 left and right; 88–9 centre; 101 below
Daily Telegraph title page (photo Bill Beck)
Enell Inc. 55
The Executors of 'Vicky' half-title page
Express Newspapers Ltd 34 left
John Freeman 24
Giles 100
Granada 72; 74 left and right; 75 above
Heath 101 above
Keystone Press 64 left, above and below; 65 right, above; 75 right, below

Jan Lukas 108 above and below
Ministry of Information 36
Mirrorpic 70 left and right; 71 right (photo Eugene Hackley)
The Observer/Jane Bown 103; 106 below
PAP 82 right, below
Stephen Peet 81 above and below
Planet News 66 below; 88 left, above
Private Eye 76
Punch 62
Zev Radovan 93 (courtesy *The Universe*)
Scripture Union 94
Sunday Times 91
Time Inc. 85 left and right
'Trog' 111

The photographs not otherwise credited are drawn from the author's private collection, with the exception that those in the 'Park Cottage' section (p.116ff) are by Chris Barham, who also took the photograph of Kitty Muggeridge on p.25, that of the montage on pp.52–3, and 'An Evening with Malcolm Muggeridge' on p.83 (above).

Index